PRAISE FOR *DISCIPLES OF THE NATIONS*

"Paul Sungro Lee's book shows how to do mission well, drawing on theory, international teaching experience, and extensive personal field experience. Both gospel and culture are taken seriously in this text, and passion brings it to life."

—MIRIAM ADENEY
former President, American Society of Missiology, and Associate Professor of World Christian Studies, Seattle Pacific University

"Here is a unique and relevant volume, bringing together elements of thoughtful memoir, missions theory, and practical training.... Readers will be grateful to find that the writing is accessible and the advice is eminently practical."

—STEPHEN T. PARDUE
Associate Professor of Theology, Asia Graduate School of Theology, and co-editor of Majority World Theology Series

"This is a fascinating autobiographical story of migration and mission told by one who has lived in three continents. It is also full of wisdom about missionary discipleship, to which it brings a different global perspective from most comparable works."

—KIRSTEEN KIM
Paul E. Pierson Chair in World Christianity and Associate Dean for the Center for Missiological Research, Fuller Theological Seminary

"This book is more than a perfunctory reading of theological abstractions on cross-cultural missions. Honest reflections on his own life and those whom God has called, and is calling, Dr. Lee to serve, this book paints a vivid picture of the power of the gospel to change lives, one person, one group at a time. This book will compel and prepare readers and missional leaders to seek and follow the Holy Spirit—into uncharted waters of redemption, restoration, and reconciliation."

—LOUIS WILSON
Senior Pastor, New Song Community Church, Baltimore, Maryland

"This book will not only rekindle our love for God and God's people but will also challenge us to take Matthew 28:19 seriously as Dr. Lee does."

—Danny C. S. Ro
 Senior Pastor, Sarang Community Church of Southern California, Anaheim, California

"*Disciples of the Nations* presents scholarly research but remains accessibly practical. Further, it reads deeply personal, speaking to the heart and inspiring action.... It is a long-awaited resource for the global church."

—Sadiri Joy Tira
 Lausanne Movement Senior Associate and Catalyst for Diasporas, Canada

"Dr. Paul Lee, who we have known and highly esteemed for many years, writes what he has lived and we have seen the undeniable hand of God upon both his teaching and those who have learned from him."

—Les Norman
 Founder, DCI Global Partnerships, United Kingdom

"Dr. Lee offers solid missiological insight birthed out of both his academic understanding of world missions and, more importantly, years of practicing incarnational ministry in a variety of international contexts. His writing serves as a valuable resource for those training to serve internationally as well as those who are currently navigating the complexities of intercultural discipleship."

—Chad Williams
 Senior Pastor, Union Church of Manila, Philippines

"This book is brimming with rich biblical insights gleaned from years of scholarly research and fruitful missionary work in three continents. I highly recommend this for every serious follower of Christ who wants to be more effective in discipling men and women in different multicultural contexts."

—Tom Roxas
 President, International Graduate School of Leadership, Philippines

"Dr. Lee presents honest reports on discipleship in the cross-cultural context of both cases of success and failure. . . . Not just theological principles but much practical missionary experiences are felt to make his book a wonderful symphony. This book is an excellent guide for pastors and missionaries to evaluate their work and for ministry interns to discover their models."
—Myung Ho Kim
    former Director, Disciple Making Ministries International, South Korea

"This book is a rare combination of personal experiences and scholarly researches. . . . Just as Mordecai described Esther's selfless ministry that blessed the people of God, I'm confident that his elaborate book is a gift to our generation 'for such a time as this.'"
—Kangchoon Lee
    General Secretary, Jesus Korea Sungkyul Church, South Korea

"Dr. Lee's book is more than just a theoretical table discussion. I trust that the Holy Spirit will enlighten you as you read through every page of his book with rich experiences and practical advice on cross-cultural discipleship. Amid the flood of writings about techniques of discipleship, his book uncompromisingly stresses the lifestyle of discipleship."
—Youn Dong Chung
    former President, Sungkyul Theological Seminary, South Korea

"I have long been interested in the origin of ideas and cross-cultural engagement. Dr. Lee invites the reader into both of these areas of my personal interest. Perhaps the central question in this book is how we as Christians can engage with those around us, while both respecting people whose beliefs and cultures differ from those of our own and at the same time, maintaining the centrality of the gospel message and confidence we have. . . . Dr. Lee really addresses a cross-cultural ministry."
—Rollin A. Van Broekhoven
    former US Federal Judge

Disciples of the Nations

ALSO BY PAUL SUNGRO LEE

*Missionary Candidate Training:
Raising Up Third World Missionaries*

Disciples of the Nations

Multiplying Disciples and Churches in Global Contexts

PAUL SUNGRO LEE

Foreword by Rollin A. Van Broekhoven

RESOURCE *Publications* · Eugene, Oregon

DISCIPLES OF THE NATIONS
Multiplying Disciples and Churches in Global Contexts

Copyright © 2021 Paul Sungro Lee. All rights reserved. Except for brief quotations in critical publications or reviews, no part of this book may be reproduced in any manner without prior written permission from the publisher. Write: Permissions, Wipf and Stock Publishers, 199 W. 8th Ave., Suite 3, Eugene, OR 97401.

This book is composed of edited transcriptions from lectures and study materials prepared by Paul Sungro Lee, PhD, at International Graduate School of Leadership, 2020.

All Scripture quotations, unless otherwise indicated, are from the Holy Bible, New International Version®, NIV®, copyright © 1973, 1978, 1984, 2011 by Biblica, Inc.™ Used by permission. All rights reserved worldwide.

Resource Publications
An Imprint of Wipf and Stock Publishers
199 W. 8th Ave., Suite 3
Eugene, OR 97401

www.wipfandstock.com

PAPERBACK ISBN: 978-1-7252-9079-2
HARDCOVER ISBN: 978-1-7252-9080-8
EBOOK ISBN: 978-1-7252-9081-5

02/23/21

To Eunice,
my loving wife and soulmate,
who showed endurance and trust of many years
in the quest for fruitful cross-cultural discipleship.
I'm deeply indebted to her ongoing support of love.

Contents

Foreword by Rollin A. Van Broekhoven　　ix
Prologue　　xiii

PART I: CALLED FROM THE NATIONS

1. Tugging of God　　3
2. Potter's Molding Hand　　12
3. Africa? No Way!　　16
4. Asian Tigers and Global Expansion　　22

PART II: CALLED INTO THE NATIONS

5. Multiplying Disciples in Cross-Cultural Contexts　　29
6. The Holy Spirit, Mastermind of World Mission　　56
7. Mobilizing Missionaries from the Nations　　62

PART III: CALLED FOR THE NATIONS

8. Worldview Matters　　83
9. Contextualization Is at Hand　　98

PART IV: DESIRE OF THE NATIONS

10. Cultural Homogenization and Incarnation　　117
11. Missionary Paternalism　　132
12. The Church Construction Model on the Mission Field　　139
13. The Final Frontier　　148

Epilogue　　154
Bibliography　　161
Subject Index　　167

Foreword

Dr. Paul Sungro Lee has written a book that strikes many chords, many of which reach my mind and heart at different levels. By way of background, I have known Dr. Lee for many years, although, to my loss, have not followed him and his work closely. Oh, we have kept in touch over the years and I had some general idea of where he was and what he was doing.

So, perhaps I should start here where I started: reading the book. *Memoir*, French for memory, implies what one contemporary writer described as a "looser form of self-reflection, a more experiential and impressionistic sketch of one's past" and "their impact is all the more felt due to their capacity to speak to emotion, mystery, and faith." As my friend Professor James Houston wrote in his memoir, for Christians memoirs are far more profound expressions of self-reflection because in writing them we also stand before God.[1]

To make it clear to the reader, Dr. Lee has not written an autobiography, although much of what he has written has a certain autobiographical ring that comes from his experience as a missionary in Africa and Asia, and a life of training in the United States. Although I knew him as a doctoral student, as I read this book, I realized that I really did not know him at all. Moreover, there is nothing in this book that is egotistical or narcissistic. There is nothing to satisfy my curiosity or that of others. He leaves that to another generation.

I have long been interested in the origin of ideas and cross-cultural engagement. Dr. Lee invites the reader into both of these areas of my personal interest. Perhaps the central question in this book is how we as Christians can engage with those around us, while both respecting people whose beliefs and cultures differ from those of our own and, at the same time, maintaining the centrality of the gospel message and confidence we have. While not directly pertinent here to our current situation in the United States with political divisions and racial strife, those of us who have lived and

---

1. Houston, *Memoirs of a Joyous Exile*.

traveled widely around the world often find ourselves exploring how people find common ground across deep and sometimes painful differences. It is true that Dr. Lee does not dwell on the exploration of common ground across deep and sometimes painful differences. The perceptive reading of the experiences of a missionary from Korea who immigrated to the United States with his parents, trained in the United States, and then engaged in Kenya and surrounding areas in Africa as a missionary for sixteen years gives us the hint of cultural engagement in discipleship in Africa as a way of fulfilling his understanding of the Great Commission. We see how God blessed his work in Africa, taught him lessons of blessings and church growth, but also of seeming failures. But, he remained faithful to the Great Commission to disciple all nations. And then he returned to Korea before serving in the Philippines as a missionary engaged in making disciples.

However, it is far more than a memoir! While it may be true that its authenticity is derived, in part, from a life lived discipling people of all nations, it reflects a wonderful reflection on words in the Great Commission, especially to go and make disciples of all nations. This is not simply a book about church planting or church growth. Making disciples in any context may be difficult, but certainly in a culture foreign to our own. Although it may have that as a consequence of living the Great Commission, and may have that effect in one's home country, Dr. Lee really addresses a cross-cultural ministry.

To this end, as a Western-trained lawyer and educator, I am impressed by Dr. Lee's book because it is in large part directed to Western-trained educators and missionaries working in, or planning to work in, non-Western settings, primarily in making disciples to lead the church in its development and growth. It would, therefore, seem that there are several goals in mind. As Drs. Judith and Sherwood Lingenfelter[2] express this first goal, it is to help all teachers—and, I would add, missionaries—to understand their own culture of teaching and learning.

The second point I would make is that a second goal is to equip teachers, preachers, missionaries, church planters and leaders to become effective learners in another cultural context with the specific focus on church planting and church growth. To this end, Dr. Lee applied his learning as he discipled church leaders. But, as he readily admits in his book, not all models were successful.

While it may be the case that much of his experience as described in his book addresses that goal, a third point I would make from my reading of the manuscript is that what Dr. Lee writes helps church leaders and church

---

2. Lingenfelter and Lingenfelter, *Teaching Cross-Culturally*.

planters reflect on the cultural differences and conflicts they might have with others as they use the perspective of the Scripture and faith in Jesus Christ. Again, as Drs. Judith and Sherwood Lingenfelter express, the Bible gives principles for living that transcend culture, but we often miss these because of our cultural blindness.

The fourth goal is rather simple. The idea here is that church leaders and church planters working outside their home culture enjoy their teaching and discipleship-making experience and feel that they are helping those to whom they have dedicated their lives.

It is clear that Dr. Lee has worked for many years in many non-Western contexts and cultures. While there is an academic quality to his writing, particularly derived from his postgraduate education and experience in the United States, what comes through so clearly is his heart for ministry and especially for the church. It also is clear that he has experienced much of what he has written. Moreover, what Dr. Lee writes in an international context is equally valid on a national level to those of us in some leadership role in our respective churches who work to build the church as integral to the kingdom of God. If done properly, our work should also influence the cultures in which we find ourselves, because that is the nature of God's kingdom on earth.

HON. ROLLIN A. VAN BROEKHOVEN, JD, LLM, PHD, DLITT, DPS, LLD

Former U.S. Federal Judge, Former Board Chair of Evangelical Council for Financial Accountability, Visiting Scholar at University of Oxford / Centre for Socio-Legal Studies (UK), International Law Professor at China University of Political Science and Law (China)

Prologue

When I first wrote *Missionary Candidate Training: Raising Up Third World Missionaries*, I had the dimmest clue that it would be translated into the major world languages and put into use in various churches and schools of the Majority World as their missionary training text. It has encouraged me to carry out this daunting task of a book writing again. Since then, further and deeper investigations have been articulated in the quest for fruitful cross-cultural discipleship and church planting that might work in global contexts.

I'm a firm believer in cross-cultural discipleship. I also believe in the Great Commission, which should be a life mandate and practice of everyone who professes Christ as Lord and Savior. Having lived and ministered for equal portions in Asia, America, and Africa and seen God using this scared, reluctant, and introverted man and my international team to disciple Christian leaders of all ages and to plant over three hundred churches to impact fifteen nations of Africa and Asia for nearly a quarter-century in partnership with organizations like the Christian and Missionary Alliance, among a dozen others, my conviction became solid. Nevertheless, I didn't want to merely share my experience but to validate it through research. Hence, the research reflected in this book has been scientifically validated to provide objective data for the readers. This book aims to help readers grasp a sense of real, tangible missionary work.

All in all, this is a byproduct of my love story with Jesus, who found me years ago while I was still seeking God and life purpose. I've sensed God's unchanging love throughout my life despite all my shortcomings and mistakes. He is the one I wish to magnify in this book, not anyone else. I pray you will likewise sense his love as you go through the pages. This book is, by no means, a complete reference for world mission. Yet, it is my humble prayer that this mere collection of my experience and research in Africa and Asia may serve as a reminder that God is still willing and able to use *anyone* who is committed to following him and his mandate to "go and make disciples of all nations" (Matthew 28:19). It portrays a confirmed life story of a man and his co-laborers who endeavored to follow Christ in the United States, Kenya, South Korea, and the Philippines. Readers will, of course, need to transliterate the contents into their own time and space to make it more relevant to suit the contextualized demands of one's community.

I must mention that I'm deeply grateful to Les Norman, whose visionary work and humble life in Nottingham, England, has served as an example of a disciple-maker for the nations and inspired many around the world. Hosung Maeng of rMaeng2 and Wipf and Stock Publishers has helped the publication of this book in every way. His continuous support and motivation are saturated in every page of this book. A good portion of the book content came from what I taught at the International Graduate School of Leadership and other Christian and Missionary Alliance–related seminaries around the world. My students helped me acquire valuable missiological insights since they represented fairly over twenty nationalities, many of whom came to study from the Creative Access Regions. Numerous disciples of the nations of past, present, and future—they are my inspiration, source, and reason for this book.

Paul Sungro Lee
March 2020

PART I

Called from the Nations

1

Tugging of God

LEARNING YEARS

> But you stay here with me so that I may give you all the commands, decrees and laws you are to teach them to follow in the land I am giving them to possess. (Deuteronomy 5:32)

It is one thing for someone to love football and play it for a hobby; it's another thing for him to play football for living as a professional. Certainly, there is a different level of commitment involved. The former may not need to go through extra challenges and hardships of training but just indulge in the excitement of the sport. However, the latter should seriously consider various factors involved in his career and dauntlessly welcome both the pros and cons of commitment. Likewise, I tend to perceive that knowing "about" missions somewhat differs from knowing missions. This book was written with that principle in mind. After all, it is a blend of research and fieldwork.

God impressed upon my heart many years ago what has become a significant initiative of this book. I have witnessed discipleship multiplied in chains at parachurch ministries like Cru (also known as Campus Crusade for Christ), which has its presence in some 190 countries.[1] I've also learned the same principle working in local church settings when I attended the Called to Awaken the Laity seminar of Disciple Making Ministries International in cooperation with Sarang Community Church, one of the

---

1. Goodstein, "Campus Crusade for Christ Is Renamed."

largest Presbyterian churches in the world with sixty thousand members in Seoul, Korea.[2] However, I desired to see if the multiplication of discipleship could also take place in cross-cultural contexts. I believe I have read virtually every book on cross-cultural discipleship. On top of what the Lord has taught me through those wonderful learning experiences I mentioned, the greatest source of learning, testing, and validation came from what God has been doing through the Evangelical Alliance for Preacher Training/Commission (EAPTC) in diverse parts of the world since 1996. My cross-cultural encounters in Africa and Asia while working with EAPTC virtually paved the way. I have still tarried many years to write this book because I wanted to put into practice firsthand what I was theorizing and see if it indeed worked on the field. I desired it to be a balanced attempt of both orthodoxy (right thinking) and orthopraxis (right practice) in the world mission effort. I wanted to know what I was talking about.

CROSSING CULTURES

> . . . Make disciples of *all nations* . . . (Matthew 28:19)

The Holy Spirit, the Mastermind behind every missionary works, still does make disciples of *all nations*. He is calling you today to labor with him for this honorable yet inevitable task—either by sending or by going. But the foremost task remains. How will you incubate all the *nations* in your heart first so that you may go and make disciples?

It was one sunny yet chilly spring afternoon in the 1980s that I was called by my high school teacher at her office back in the western United States. One of my subject teachers sternly rebuked me and said, "You don't seem to be paying attention to my words. I rarely see you making eye contact with me both in classes and in private meetings." I inhaled deeply, suspecting that my body language had been utterly misunderstood by my teacher, who must have had a genuine concern for me.

My family had just immigrated to a suburban Denver, Colorado, from South Korea. My father found a new job at a local factory while my mother started working at a nearby hotel gift shop. I was enrolled at a public high school and soon found out that I was the only kid who didn't speak in English in the entire school. My younger brother had even harder times to adjust to his new junior high school. All Lees were struggling in this new settlement that they just ventured into in the United States.

---

2. Zaimov, "S. Korean Megachurch Pastor Loses Case."

Ironically, my parents did not inform me and my brother earlier about our immigration plan until it reached only two weeks before departure, fearing that we might stop studying hard and become slack and possibly drop out of school in Korea. We were unprepared for what was about to come! Suddenly, I became a fresh immigrant trying to settle in different environments, which I've never been previously exposed to. Apart from language acquisition, I was besieged with many new American cultures that I had to familiarize myself with.

One of them was my behavior toward teachers. Back then, it was unthinkable for me to look at authority figures eye to eye, having been accustomed to Asian cultures. Any decent Asian boy and girl would be expected to avoid direct eye contact with teachers and to stare ten to fifteen degrees below their eyes as a sign of respect toward elders. I was crossing cultures, and it wasn't easy.

In late 2001, I traveled to Burkina Faso, a landlocked West African country, to minister at a pastors' seminar in the capital city of Ouagadougou. My wife, Eunice, and I had worked as missionaries in Kenya for years by then. I thought I had become quite acquainted with ardent African worship style—but not with this one. There I saw a group of attendees who were praising God by clapping their hands vertically rather than horizontally! It was one bewildering scene, at least to me. Moreover, I soon felt like an odd one out because I kept clapping my hands horizontally while most did so vertically during the praise session. Psalm 47:1 instructs us by saying, "Clap your hands, all you nations. Shout to God with the voice of triumph." However, the Bible does not specify how to clap our hands. Crossing cultures certainly has many learning curves.

Eunice and our two children relocated with me to the Philippines in 2016 to team up with the International Graduate School of Leadership (IGSL), which Bill Bright founded in Manila for Christian leadership training. In one of those early days of our adjustment to Manila life, my son, Titus, came home for dinner after playing basketball with Filipino kids in the neighborhood. Somewhat displeased, he began to share about his basketball match at the dinner table. "Dad, it was kind of awkward. Those Filipino guys were trying to kiss me at the match!" Eunice and I were confused (and frankly concerned) about exactly what had happened that day and decided to investigate further the very next day. As we obscurely guessed, we soon discovered that it was a Filipino way of pointing directions with a lip that Titus encountered during the game. We couldn't help but laugh only to learn that those kids were pointing to Titus where to pass the ball! He was obviously unaware of such a cultural distinctive. Crossing from one culture to another surely requires adequate preparations.

First Timothy 2:4 confirms that God's heart desires *all* men to be saved and to come to the knowledge of the truth. Making disciples in cross-cultural contexts has been both my life and struggle, which has made me continue to research and experiment as a scholar-practitioner of world mission. I've attempted to approach sound intercultural lifestyle in its relation to the biblical world mission in this writing. Heaven will be a place of diversity. We'd better get used to it first from this side of eternity.

UNSEEN HAND

My intercultural life story began with the unseen hand of God orchestrating the whole panorama on the backstage. Before I came to the Philippines, I had lived approximately a third of my life in Korea, the next third in the United States, and the other third in Kenya. I would have never dreamt nor planned such a roller coaster on my pathway. It certainly took a tender leading of the Master's hand to guide me so.

I was born into a family with strong Confucian beliefs and minor Buddhist practices. Neither of these religions quenched my spiritual fervor in childhood. It was in my teenage years that I was led by a friend to attend church. He didn't exactly lead me to Christ, but somehow enticed me to some girls in the church youth group, whom I initially found more appealing. During the 70s and 80s, South Korea was passing the pinnacle of national revival and church growth. A native of South Korea, one of the blessings I've witnessed was to see firsthand some of those megachurches with unprecedented quantitative church growth in history, riding on the wave of nationwide revival. Though somewhat controversial with the means to measure the true size of churches, it is undeniable that South Korea still dominates a chart of some of the largest congregations in the world. Many gospel rallies, often citywide, were held in those days of my youth. One day I found out that one of the girls I was pursuing in the youth group was going to a gospel rally. I was naturally inclined to follow her to the meeting.

While my sole interest at that time was to win the heart of this girl, I cringed at the size of the crowd. It was a massive meeting, possibly tens of thousands gathered from all corners of Seoul. I could barely see the preacher from a distance where I was seated. Still baffled by this new experience, the preacher's voice unexpectedly lit a beacon into my soul. He asserted that out of God's love Jesus came to die for my sins and to give me a new life. It suddenly dawned on me. I had never heard in Buddhism that Buddha loved me so much that he died in my place. Not a single time I could recall that Confucius loved me to the point of dying for me, let alone anyone. My heart was greatly stirred to wonder why then this Jesus would do such a strange thing for me when I did not even ask for it. It was a revolutionary message to me. Moreover, I had always wanted to live a meaningful life and thus thought Jesus could help me live it. The message of the cross captivated my soul. Why could a stranger take the place of my punishment and love me through such a horrible execution? The Son of God extended his invitation for me to accept his love and will in my life and a chance to live most meaningfully by following him. It was on that day the God I'd been searching for met me in person and showed me what my life and I were worthy of. I realized that I was worthy of the cost of the life of God's Son. With tears rolling on my cheek, I found myself responding to the preacher's call to pray to invite Jesus into my life. It was one unforgettable day that only what would come afterward would show me the true meaning of.

FROM ASIA TO AMERICA

I wasn't yet sure of what God would have me to do in my life even after that extraordinary day. I still struggled to find a clear purpose in my life. Challenges in studies, peer pressures in and out of school, and temptations from the surroundings did not fade away. But two things were obviously different. I never suffered again from constant nightmares, which had kept disturbing me now and then before I invited Jesus into my life. I was free from those horrendous night haunters. My fears were drowned in the perfect love of Christ. Besides, I began to sense the gentle tugging of God's unseen hand at every turn of my life. It was initially surreal but it always came with strong convictions. It began to dawn on me that it was God calling me and preparing me for what he would have me to do for the nations in the years to come.

Jesus was constantly knocking at the door of my heart from the early days of my life. I can recall that there was always a Christian friend, teacher, or neighbor whom God used to draw me closer to him. Even after having encountered Christ in my life, his tugging continued. From the moments when I was tempted to sin to the times when I needed strength to get up on my feet again from setbacks, he was there for me.

> Here I am! I stand at the door and knock. If anyone hears my voice and opens the door, I will come in and eat with that person, and they with me. (Revelation 3:20)

My teenage years as a new immigrant in the U.S. began rather dumbfounded. Often frustrated and discouraged, I was drawn nearer to the

Lord each time I felt downcast. I had surrendered the control of my youthful passion to Christ. Amid many challenging circumstances, unexplainable joy began to overflow my soul every day, and I couldn't help but share the gospel with my family and my high school rosters. "Joy is the most infallible sign of the presence of God,"[3] Pierre de Chardin once said. That immense joy is what captivated my soul and energized my day-to-day life. One by one, within two years my family also came to the knowledge of the Savior. From family to friends, I found it exhilarating to tell others about the Lord whom I met and who leads the steps of my life.

As the number of friends in my high school coming to the Lord increased, a praise band was formed for greater outreach, which later became known as the *Psalm 150* ministry. The group was mostly composed of my high school friends who used to be rockers, drug addicts, and even gang members, and experienced dramatic transformation after finding Jesus. We shared the gospel one on one at our schools on weekdays and frequently performed at local churches on weekends. I saw this group leading over three hundred high school students in my town by the time I left for college. It was an amazing adventure! I felt I had embarked on what God had in store for my life calling.

FIRST LOVE

In those years, I fell in love with Jesus for the first time. I was in a spiritual honeymoon with the Lord. First love was ignited. Telling others about the invisible God who so loved me became my daily practice. At the same time, I was anxiously searching for what God would want me to do for life.

During my childhood, I desired to become an artist, mostly because I loved art and was quite good at it. A thought of entering the money-generating realty business also grasped my heart for a while in my earlier years of American life. Even after surrendering my life to follow Christ, I never dreamt of becoming a missionary to reach the nations. Serving the Lord in local contexts would be more than enough, I thought.

One day I was reading through the Bible, following my daily devotional calendar. This verse serendipitously popped up to pierce my heart.

> What good will it be for someone to gain the whole world, yet forfeit their soul? Or what can anyone give in exchange for their soul? (Matthew 16:26)

---

3. This quote is drawn from Velick, *Joy!*.

After describing the cost of following him and carrying one's cross, Jesus laid out the meaning of possibly the best life one could live out. That is to save one's own soul and, in turn, to be used by God for others to do the same. Jesus repeats the same question in Mark 8:36 and Luke 9:25. Deeply sunken into this life-changing inspiration, it slowly but surely dawned on me that dedicating my life for soul-winning would be more meaningful than cherishing my petty ambition to pursue a comfortable life. It was my initial desire to somehow make good money, retire early, enjoy the rest of my life by traveling the world, and hopefully live healthily and die later without sickness. When this grand "kingdom dream" was incubated in me, my so-called American dream seemed so tiny and fractional. The confession of C. T. Studd often made my heart resonate in those early days.

> If Jesus Christ be God and died for me, *then no sacrifice can be too great for me to make for Him.*

AMERICAN DREAM OR KINGDOM DREAM

I knew I would be answerable to Jesus on those disturbing and unavoidable issues. The spiritual honeymoon period slowly faded away. The testing period of my faith and commitment arrived. I had to choose between the American dream and the kingdom dream. The Lord kept wrestling with me about the purpose of life in those days. My existence seemed so tiny and insignificant in this universe, like sand on the seashore that comes today and will be swept away tomorrow by the waves of history. I did not want to waste my life, which Jesus purchased with his sacrificial love. Would my life be counted worthwhile? Would I have lived a life of positive influence on others? Would my life be pleasing to God? What would the life God wants from me look like? Such meaningful questions lingered in my soul. The Lord Jesus guided me again with this scripture.

> The thief does not come except to steal, and to kill, and to destroy. I have come that they may have life, and that they may have it more abundantly. (John 10:10)

There are people whose lives are lived to steal, kill, and destroy others. People are hurting because of their life. Jesus was challenging me to pursue the life of following his footsteps. I was challenged again to make my goalpost a life that makes other people live an abundant life and that, in turn, makes this world a better place. At the prevailing thought that I'm renting this life from Christ with a lease that expires in about eighty years, I knew

I'd have to wisely set a course of my life. What would remain after my time on earth is over? A deep contemplation led me to figure that I'd be able to leave two things behind: first, the cause of Christ, and second, people I've influenced for it. I had to rearrange my priorities in line with these criteria. Finance, education, time, relationship—everything had to be aligned to this new worldview. That was the clincher. Surprisingly, it wasn't quite difficult. Once this worldview was engraved in my soul, the rest of the pieces of life details came to find their matches to complete the puzzle of life.

> Of what use is money in the hand of a fool, since he has no desire to get wisdom? (Proverbs 17:16)

The Lord knew that only dreams with eternal value would bequeath the true meaning of life and produce indestructible happiness in the process. It is no wonder that "we are materially so much better off than we were 50 years ago, but we're not one iota happier," said Chris Peterson, a psychology professor at the University of Michigan.[4] I chose to pursue the kingdom dream. I sensed God's tugging to dedicate my life to serve in full-time ministry. I was saturated by the kingdom rationales. God's faithful seasonal leadings toward it have won me over. A life dedicated to making disciples of the nations has been worth it. It is worth it indeed. Besides, I've been happy to walk on this path for well over three decades by now. As I wished earlier, people of far and near have found a better life on account of me. Most of all, God is magnified in my life. This is the life I dreamt about.

Following Christ and making disciples of all nations is God's command. Those who obey get to find genuine meaning and happiness in life. That is God's unchanging promise.

> "If you, Israel, will return, then return to me," declares the Lord.
> "If you put your detestable idols out of my sight and no longer go astray, and if in a truthful, just and righteous way you swear, 'As surely as the Lord lives,' then the nations will invoke blessings by him and in him they will boast." (Jeremiah 4:1–3)

DISCUSSION AND REFLECTION QUESTIONS

1. Is your life pursuing the kingdom dream, which Christ laid out in the Scriptures for a life with meaning, or is it pursuing just your dream?

---

4. Farino, "How Happy Is Your City?"

2. Have you previously experienced any challenges in dealing with different cultures? How could you have done it differently?
3. Is your life making a positive difference in this world? Is your world becoming a better place because of your existence on earth?

2

Potter's Molding Hand

LIFE OF NOT MY OWN

It was a hot and scorching summer day in 1993. I was studying at a Bible college in Oklahoma to prepare for ministry and eventually to be ordained as a minister. I traveled back to Colorado to see my parents during a summer break. I wasn't exactly clear about God's direction in my future ministry. I spent a week of fasting and prayer at a solitary retreat cabin on Rocky Mountain. Desperate and hungry for God's will for my life, I was ready for anything God would have in store for me. Weak in body yet alert in spirit near the end of that week, the Lord impressed on my heart what would become a life vision.

> Build me the church, which will bring millions into my presence, on the Word and power.

I shook to the core of my entire being. I knew I had heard from God. But it seemed so vague back then. To be frank, I was quite scared of what would come of my future. With this call, it had become evident that my life was not my own. The Designer had his purpose, and I knew I was to fulfill that grand purpose by setting aside all my personal ambitions. When this life vision was cast on me that day on a foothill of Rocky Mountain, I was convinced I should have no reservation. The words of 1 Corinthians 6:19-20 kept echoing in my soul for weeks after this encounter.

> Do you not know that your bodies are the temples of the Holy Spirit, who is in you, whom you have received from God? You are not your own; you were bought at a price. Therefore honor God with your bodies.

After all, an adventurous journey of many unexpected excitements began. It was only a beginning.

PEOPLE OF NOT MY OWN

South Korea, my birthplace, stands out as one of few racially homogeneous nations. I'd never faced a foreigner in person back in my childhood in Korea. I could see people of different skin colors, languages, and cultures only on TV and movies. It wasn't a comfortable setting for me at all to learn to live with people from diverse cultures in the melting pot society of America. I had no idea that the Lord was teaching me a lesson in those days to familiarize myself with the ministry for people not of my own.

One of the reasons I believe Jesus chose to live as a carpenter in his earthly life was because carpenters normally work with three major tools everyday: nails, timbers, and hammers. He lived with them for nearly thirty years. Those three tools were the very mechanisms by which he would die for the sins of the world. He lived to die for us. Perhaps he was constantly reminding himself of his call by living in such an environment. This tells us even today that if you prayerfully reflect your past and the way you have walked by now, you can possibly see a hint of your call. If you contemplate your childhood and the way you were brought up in luxury or austerity, there is probably an answer. There might be some footprints of the Lord that have been guiding you throughout.

The Lord was using each life segment to call me and prepare me to serve the nations, not just my own people. Making disciples in cross-cultural contexts has motivated me to keep researching and experimenting in this discipline. It took years for me to learn that *people are people*. God never made Americans, Chinese, Filipinos, etc. He simply made a man and a woman! Every people group existing today has derived from Adam and Eve as the Bible affirms. Because we have lived for so long far away from one another, we began to look different and speak differently.

> From one man he made all the nations, that they should inhabit the whole earth; and he marked out their appointed times in history and the boundaries of their lands. (Acts 17:26)

As long as we see foreigners as different "species," it may be difficult for us to discover common triggers to authentically connect with them. When we acknowledge the divine connectivity of all human beings in this biblical reflection, we create a bonding through which cultures can be legitimately crossed. In his contributing article to Global Diasporas and Mission, Amos Yong wrote that diasporas capture the very heart of God's saving work regardless of their time, place, and people group.[1] I sensed there was a reason God made me who I am—a cultural hybrid.

INTO ANOTHER POT

At first, I did not want to get involved in cross-cultural ministry. It would certainly mean living out of my comfort zone, like often going without water or electricity, drinking water of doubtful sources at times, eating foods of unpleasant smell and taste, sleeping on uncomfortable beddings, wrestling with all kinds of vermin and possible malaria and dengue, living with the constant vulnerability of possible robbery and pickpockets as a foreigner, and of course, needless to say, ongoing exposure to risks and dangers from trips, like unpredictability and hostility. Who would like this kind of life? And who would want to marry a man like that? Those were the preliminary questions in my mind while I was still dedicating my life to world mission as a single man. Nevertheless, Jesus implied that we should count the cost when he said "go" and make disciples of all nations.

The Lord Jesus was there with me when a group of policemen raided for interrogation in the middle of my preaching at a house church in China. I know he was there with me inside a war-torn village house in the Democratic Republic of Congo when I went there to speak at a Bible school graduation. As I traveled the four corners of the world to tell others about Christ's love and message, he has been with me through it all just as he promised in Matthew 18:20: ". . . surely I am with you always." I learned by experience that one of the surest ways to sense God's presence is to live out a life of missions. The Lord has been undeniably faithful to me despite my occasional doubts and passive obedience.

Even while at a Bible college, I wasn't fully willing to engage in full-time missionary work. I had a hunch that the Lord wanted to use me for missions but my heart was leaning toward a comfortable home assignment rather than "going" as I was about to leave the college. The Lord had to form me into another pot in the years to come, shaping me as seemed best to him. I felt like the apostle Paul when the Holy Spirit would not allow

---

1. Im and Yong, *Global Diasporas and Mission*, 261.

him and his team to enter Bithynia but detoured them to Macedonia (Acts 16:6–10). Open doors for ministry opportunities I pursued ended up closing at every corner no matter how promising they looked at first. I sensed frustrations and despairs everywhere I turned to ignore God's call to missionary involvement. I felt broken and unfulfilled after a while. Brokenheartedness is the prerequisite of a Christian leader's heart (Psalm 34:18). Brokenheartedness nourishes one's desperation toward the Lord and his attitude of constant self-examination, and ultimately initiates him to give God the glory for works he does through him. God had to break me first so that he might mold me into a useful instrument for his purpose.

> But the pot he was shaping from the clay was marred in his hands; so the potter formed it *into another pot*, shaping it as seemed best to him. (Jeremiah 18:4)

Now as I reflect on the unseen hand of the Lord having lovingly molded me at every stage, I can surely testify that his goodness and love have followed me all the days of my life and, undoubtedly, will continue to do so (Psalm 23:6). I had actually preached more in English than in my native tongue by this time. It was an act of God. The Holy Spirit graciously started his work in me to write out a beautiful story of his goodness and mercy.

DISCUSSION AND REFLECTION QUESTIONS

1. Take a moment to contemplate how the invisible hand of God has guided and shaped you up to this time. Can you recall the moments that you sensed the undeniable presence of God in your life? If so, please list them.

2. Upon reflection of your past and the way you have walked until now, can you see a hint of your call? Examining the footprints of the Lord left on the pathway of your past will help project your future call.

3. Do you believe that your life is currently in alignment with God's will? If not, what could you do differently to change that?

3

Africa? No Way!

STARRY NIGHT IN KENYA

It happened while I was at a remote village in western Kenya for a preaching trip in 1996. I had just embarked on a career in missionary work in Africa. I was staying at the house of a local pastor who invited me to come and speak for his congregation. In the middle of the night, I woke up to use a latrine outside of the house. As soon as I stepped out of the house, I couldn't help but stop for a while at the awe of a bright moon and starry night sky. Suddenly, I sensed the Lord whispering this statement into my soul: "Your disciples will be as many as those stars . . ." Following that heart-leaping encounter, I lapsed into meditation on God's promise to Abraham in Genesis 15:5 in the weeks to come: "He took him outside and said, 'Look up at the sky and count the stars—if indeed you can count them.' Then he said to him, 'So shall your offspring be.'"

We read in the Bible that God reaffirmed his promise to Abraham time and time again. However, the very first time recorded in the Bible that God spoke to Abraham was in Genesis 12:1–3. There God assures his covenant to him by repeating the famous "I will" statements. He promises that he will show him the direction, make him into a great nation, bless him and his colleagues, curse his enemy, and eventually bless all peoples on earth through him. Most non-Jews do not have a blood-related relationship to Abraham. However, Romans 4:11–12 states that Abraham is the father of faith to both Jews and Gentiles:

> *And he received circumcision as a sign, a seal of the righteousness that he had by faith while he was still uncircumcised. So then, he is the father of all who believe but have not been circumcised, in order that righteousness might be credited to them. And he is then also the father of the circumcised who not only are circumcised but who also follow in the footsteps of the faith that our father Abraham had before he was circumcised.*

The Bible, therefore, affirms that anyone who follows Christ's way is considered Abraham's spiritual descendant as one imitates him in the growth of their faith. Abraham was to be a sampler or pathfinder of our faith. So is God's promise of Genesis 12:1–3 to him. It is our promise, too.

This classic missions mandate of the centuries-old Abrahamic blessing is based upon our total dependency on God and God alone: ". . . Go from your country, your people and your father's household to the land I will show you" (Genesis 12:1). Our country, our people, and our family and relatives are naturally the three major sources of our dependency. The initial step for Abrahamic blessing is not to develop a sense of dependency on any of those visible matters. Just like someone leaving his country for missionary service, the invisible God should be taken as the focus of our daily and lifetime dependency.

Moreover, here is the danger. Too often, we become fascinated by the part where God promises to bless us. We should never forget that all of God's blessings on our life are given for a specific purpose, as clearly articulated at the end of this Abrahamic blessing: "And *all the peoples on earth* will be blessed through you."

There're two major vocabularies for blessing in the Bible: ευλογία (*eulogia*) in Greek and בְּרָכָה (*beracha*) in Hebrew. Both imply the outward nature of the biblical blessing. God's definition of blessing is always to flow into and through you to reach others. This outward nature of God's blessing naturally creates a community of the kingdom lifestyle. It was an underlying philosophy of the early church as everyone willingly shared their skills, possessions, and expertise with others. It was an extension of heaven on earth. After living in Africa for sixteen years, I'm well aware that Africa's real problem is not poverty. Africa is one of the richest continents with natural resources and potential manpower. The problem is the hyper-imbalance of their distribution. The rich get richer and the poor get poorer. If every Christian in Africa adheres to and practices this biblical concept of blessing, it will be a far better place. The same goes for the Philippines, India, and Southeastern Asia at large.

A person saturated by this kingdom concept always looks out for opportunities to give and share—not to keep and grab. The person is aware that whatever was given in his charge is stewarded by God and that he'll be accountable. He knows the joy of giving and attests to Jesus' word that it is more blessed to give than to receive.

God has decided to bless the world, and he planned to use Abraham as a channel for that task. He likewise chose you to bless the world around you. You're God's instrument for his transformative plan for this world. In other words, God blesses you so that you can bless others. Let me put it this way. Your life as a Christian is set either to contribute toward blessing others and the world or simply to enjoy and keep God's blessings to yourself and just stop there. No matter who we are and what we do, getting the world blessed through us should be our highest life priority. That will, in turn, help fulfill our God-given destiny as mission-minded Christians. This is precisely what prompted me to fully commit to the lifestyle of a spiritual nomad, relocating for one career missionary assignment after another. It all began with the vision for Kenya.

DIVINE CONSPIRACY

Several years before this incident, I had participated in a short-term mission trip to Kenya in the early 90s. I was still a student at a Bible college. It was quite surreal to me because I had no idea about real Africa back then. All I thought about Africa was the exotic animal kingdom I watched on the National Geographic channel. Frankly, I possessed neither particular burden for the souls of Africa nor any passion for the continent of Africa. Whether it was serendipitous or inevitable, somewhere in my mind I wanted to test the waters and discern God's leading for me. I never thought I'd return to Africa to spend sixteen years of my life there. I thought that would only be a one-time experience.

Upon my return to the United States, the image of Africa was deeply rooted in my heart and never faded away. Rather, I sensed God increasing an unprecedented burden in me toward the people of Africa. I wanted to deny it in the first place. Having assumed that I had to leave my aging parents and affluent American lifestyle behind, I was making every excuse not to go to Africa. But I knew I had to eventually decide against my nature. Gentle and resilient tuggings of God to send me to Africa kept me sullen for an extended period. Soon I learned that my procrastination on the call for Africa was futile. Again, the Lord, who is full of lovingkindness and knows the best plan for my life, won my heart over with the assurance of this scripture: "... I know the plans I have for you ... plans to prosper you and not to harm you, plans to give you hope and a future" (Jeremiah 29:11). I couldn't help but surrender again and say, "Lord, not my will, but your will be done."

God had a sense of humor. In early 1996, several local churches in the U.S. came together to form a mission-sending agency, and I was interviewed and selected to be their first missionary for a field assignment in Africa. That was the very inception of the world mission outreach that is now known as the Evangelical Alliance for Preacher Training/Commission. Sent by EAPTC, I was on my way back to Kenya in the same year.

FROM AMERICA TO AFRICA

My first four years as a young missionary was full of learning curves. I was often afflicted with malaria and typhoid. The rubber met the road when my interpersonal relationship with other missionaries in the team was challenged. The first two years on the field as a single male missionary added inward loneliness on the list of turbulence.

Despite the ongoing challenges, the work grew, and I was traveling in various regions of Kenya and Uganda to meet the training needs of church leaders. God's grace was prevalent in many ways. My initial assignment on the field was mainly threefold: leadership training, social outreach, and church planting.

One of the greatest needs in Africa was for trained church leaders. EAPTC was set to fulfill the Great Commission by raising Christian leaders to take the gospel to the nations. The organization upheld an ethos based on Romans 10:8–15, which affirms that a key to the world evangelization lies in raising and sending preachers to all corners of the world. For this reason, a number of church leadership training programs were adopted and developed to meet the training needs of various types of Christian leaders. EAPTC opened its training center in Nairobi, the capital of Kenya, which later multiplied to other regions of the country. The training was provided at the minimal cost so that anyone could afford to join. It ran transcending the denominations so it would benefit Christians from broader backgrounds. Classes convened in a small group to enhance personal interactions among teachers and students. They were conducted in flexible time settings for the convenience of those who may be already in full-time ministry or in employment. This discipleship program produced thousands of graduates who are serving today as effective bishops, pastors, evangelists, elders, deacons, and Sunday school teachers in many churches and communities both inside and outside of Kenya. For those who desired further ministry training, we offered cross-cultural missionary candidate training as well as other professional trainings.

Following this move of God, EAPTC also saw to encouraging indigenous local churches to be planted through the graduates of this training program. Later on, social outreaches like nursery schools, literature production, microfinance banking projects, radio broadcasts, and orphanages branched out of those churches to cause a long-term transformation of communities and nations.

HEAVEN'S GIFTS

Nevertheless, my health situation worsened, and one day I was diagnosed with acute dysentery. It forced me to take a short break in the U.S. While I was on recovery, I was invited to speak at a missions conference organized by a local church in Virginia. After the conference, the hosting pastor introduced me to Eunice, who had recently graduated from the Trinity Evangelical Divinity School in Illinois and was a missionary candidate herself. We talked in length, literally hours after hours. The more I conversed with her, the more I felt I could talk with this lady for the rest of my life! I've never met anyone quite like her before. Ironically, she and I came from different backgrounds, if not opposite, contrasting in many ways. She grew up as a fourth-generation Presbyterian while I'm the first convert in the entire Lee family. She was a city girl while I grew up pretty much as a country boy. While she is relationship oriented, I'm task oriented. She loves noodles. I don't. The list goes on. I ended up proposing to her after much prayerful consideration. She said yes and told me that she knew it was God's will for her to marry me, having convinced herself after a great deal of observation and prayer. There was about three months of a gap between the proposal and wedding, so we inevitably had to rely on international telephone calls and primitive emails operated by modem back then, which was just introduced in Africa, for the time we were apart between Kenya and United States. We were married in October 1998. Afterward, God gave us two boys, whom Eunice and I named Timothy and Titus. With them on my side, I continued to serve a total of sixteen years in Kenya and Africa at large. They were, and are, truly heaven's gift to me.

Along the way, God has granted me a faithful group of leaders in Africa that are vigorously reaching out to communities with the shining light of Christ. They not only represent but also have been mentoring with me 1,500 trainees discipled through the EAPTC program. It was truly a sovereign work of God when we witnessed over 200 new local churches planted in ten African states through this discipleship network since 1996. They're indeed another God-sent blessing to me.

It seemed not much, nor significant, at least in the eyes of men, when a group of seven to eight determined African disciples began to meet almost two decades ago in my small office for intentional discipleship classes. We were composed of scared, timid, distressed young men and women who were simply hungry for God to use us for his glory. Years ago, the Lord Jesus commanded me to build his church. The best was yet to come.

DISCUSSION AND REFLECTION QUESTIONS

1. Lee writes, "Our country, our people, and our family and relatives are naturally the three major sources of our dependency." Have any of those visible matters created in you a sense of dependency on them rather than the invisible God and his trustworthy promises in the Scriptures? If so, identify them, and ask the Lord to increase your faith in him and his Word instead.
2. How would you come up with your definition of biblical blessing after reading this chapter?
3. Is there any area in your life that you haven't been able to surrender yet to the Lord? Meditate on Jeremiah 29:11, and see if you can let the Lord take it over and direct it so that his maturity takes root in you.

4

Asian Tigers and Global Expansion

FROM AFRICA TO ASIA

By 2011, the work in Africa grew to intercontinental dimensions with numerous local churches, Bible training centers, and nursery schools established as the Lord blessed our efforts. The following year, in 2012, my family and I consequently decided to relocate ourselves to South Korea. Having been born in Seoul, Eunice and I thought we'd easily adjust back to the environment there, only to realize that we weren't right about that. Our hearts were still in Africa. In the beginning, Timothy and Titus used to sob in their room over the feeling that they missed their Kenyan friends whom they grew up with. It seemed we couldn't know where our "home" was anymore. We somehow felt like an "international stray." We were experiencing a "reverse culture shock." What Miriam Adeney once said flawlessly described my position: "You will never be completely at home again, because part of your heart always will be elsewhere. That is the price you pay for the richness of loving and knowing people in more than one place."[1] It was around this time that the Lord Jesus reminded me that wherever he leads me to follow is to be my home. He promised in John 14:1–7 that "the Father's house has many rooms."

Our initial plan was to stay in Korea no longer than two years until I finished conducting my doctoral research there. Again, the Lord had a different plan. I soon figured that there was another reason God led us

---

1. This quote is drawn from Adeney, *Kingdom without Borders*.

back to Korea. Along with Singapore, Taiwan, and Hong Kong, South Korea is one of the four Asian Tiger nations that have experienced growing industrialization and increasing economic development in the recent era. Moreover, South Korean Christianity was strongly established as a missionary sending base for Asia and the world.[2]

INTO ANOTHER PLAN

Today, the world mission has become increasingly the task of many national churches and believers. After our relocation to South Korea, the Lord did some unexpected things with the prediction of the twenty-first-century world missions movement. I was asked by one of my Korean disciples to get involved in a church planting work in Seoul. As you may have guessed, I taught and preached to this new church about the world missionary vision. A certain Korean Chinese family in the congregation responded to the message and eventually returned to their birthplace in China, but this time with the missionary vision. Upon their arrival in China, they organized discipleship/mission training centers in various regions of China. It was our sheer joy to see another multiplication of discipleship flame just as the Lord had inflamed it all over Africa. We were keen on the movement of the Holy Spirit and prayed that the Lord would unfold his plans to penetrate this hub of Asia with the word of the Lord.

> In this way the word of the Lord spread widely and grew in power. (Acts 19:20)

China has been on my radar and vaguely in my prayer for more than a decade alongside Africa. I was seeing China be one of the hubs for reaching Asia, as Kenya was a hub for Africa. I also sensed that the spark to bring this movement to full flame in China lied rather with the neighboring missionary giant—Korea. As the Lord used Kenyans to efficiently take the message to one neighboring country after another in Africa, many Korean missionaries were able to do the same to other neighboring Asian countries of a similar cultural zone, including China.

If the Lord gives us Africa, China, and America, we've got this world pretty much covered with the flame of discipleship, I came to believe. The Lord's vision did not stop in Africa! His truth was marching on. Hebrews 11:1 tells us that faith is confidence in what we hope for and assurance about what we do not see. I did not see with my naked eyes thousands of disciples and hundreds of churches springing up when I went over to Kenya first

2. Moon, "Missions from Korea 2016," 181–85.

time. But God put his undeniable confidence and assurance in me that the vision of that African starry night would ultimately come to pass. I began to envision additional thousands of house churches in China and other creative access nations in Asia. As long as I did not give up, I knew God would fulfill *his* dream. The Lord wanted to stretch my faith to believe for global expansion. It was about this time that the Lord gave me the following Bible verses for consecutive meditation. Interestingly, a ministry partner in England wrote an email to me the very next day and told me that he felt God wanted him to share a certain scripture with me. As you may have guessed, it was exactly the same Bible passage, Isaiah 54:2–3:

> Enlarge the place of your tent, stretch your tent curtains wide, do not hold back; lengthen your cords, strengthen your stakes. For you will spread out to the right and to the left; your descendants will dispossess nations and settle in their desolate cities.

To me, it was another confirmation from the Lord. Envisioning another great harvest in China and Asia at large, the vision for global expansion was incubated in my spirit. I was convinced that God would do what he had promised, even beyond my imagination. With faith, all things are, and will be, possible. My faith grew because we serve a limitless God. Besides, the multiplication of cross-cultural discipleship was already validated to be quite possible and realistic. Therefore, establishing a base for expansion in each cultural zone became necessary and imperative.

As a result, EAPTC teams were formed in Korea and China. I assumed the role of the international director at the affirmation of EAPTC's national directors board. Once a mighty mission sender of Asia, the Korean missionary movement was losing its strong grip on the recruitment of younger generations of missionary force in the context of stagnated church growth within the country.[3] The Church of Korea has faced a serious decline in her church membership since the turn of the twenty-first century.[4] Some suggest that the population of young adults comprises less than 5 percent of the entire Church of Korea. Blessed by God as a center of revival that stood out in the 10/40 Window, this projection meant that the future of Korean Christianity was as devastating as some other 10/40 Window countries with a lower Christian ratio. Should this vicious cycle continue for a decade or two, the Church of Korea might lose the majority of her membership by the next generation. In light of this contemporary phenomenon, EAPTC wanted to contribute toward raising future Korean missionaries. For this

---

3. Johnson and Bellofatto, *Christianity in Its Global Context*, 76.
4. Hendriks and Gwak, "Interpretation of the Recent Membership Decline."

reason, the EAPTC Korea team began to run periodical missions training for young adults. This ministry was born out of our earnest prayer for God to keep the legacy of this missionary nation and to lead the flame of the missions movement for Asia and the world.

At the same time, I traveled frequently in and out of China to equip house church leaders who had no access to adequate ministry training without compromising with the increasing communistic ideology. Albeit conducting trainings underground, hidden from surveillance of the government, which often deemed foreign missionary activity as a de-Sinicization effort, zealous church leaders flocked to the meetings from every corner. My team and I fervently served Chinese house church leaders at the risk of possible expulsion, fine, and even torture, sensing that China's open door might not last forever. Some students traveled for days by train even from other provinces to join the training. The Holy Spirit has been obviously on the move in China.

In 2016, my family and I responded again to the missionary call of International Graduate School of Leadership in Manila to train Christian leaders from well over twenty Asian countries, many of which are categorized as Creative Access Nations with some restrictions for open gospel sharing. My joy was doubled in 2019 when I learned that one of my Vietnamese students took the same discipleship training back to his own country upon graduation. Despite the government's regulative control on religious activities, this Vietnamese pastor is currently engaged in multiplying discipleship groups in the "T" city. Slowly but surely, the Great Commission is mutually taking roots in the hearts of young professionals in Vietnam.

God is fulfilling his kingdom dream. I'm one of many witnesses who are thrilled at what God is doing in this time and age for *missio Dei* ("God's mission" in Latin). Christ is raising his disciples in Africa, and now in Asia as well. I'm a witness of his marvelous deeds among the nations. This is a mere sharing of what God has been doing in Africa and Asia through his servants.

DISCUSSION AND REFLECTION QUESTIONS

1. What is your definition of home? In John 14:1–7, Jesus claims himself to be the way of life and the ultimate home for his followers. How would you alter your definition of home after pondering over Jesus' definition of home?

2. What is your reaction toward your fellow Christians under persecution? Open Doors estimated that one out of every eight believers on earth faced severe persecution in 2020.[5] What would you do if you were in their shoes? Kindly utter your prayers for them at this moment.

3. What else can you do for persecuted Christians in the world? Do you sense anything God is leading you to do on their account? If so, please list them and see what you can do for your first steps.

---

5. "2020 World Watch List Report."

PART II

Called into the Nations

5

Multiplying Disciples in Cross-Cultural Contexts

We believers have been called to preach the gospel to all corners of the earth, starting with our own Jerusalem (Acts 1:8). But, is it a realistic or even possible task? Yes, I believe so. That is why Scripture tells us in another text: ". . . Everyone who calls on the name of the Lord will be saved. How, then, can they call on the one they have not believed in? And how can they believe in the one of whom they have not heard? And how can they hear without someone preaching to them?" (Romans 10:13–14). This text instructs us that it is the *preachers* who are to bring good news to everyone who would believe and get saved. In other words, the key to world evangelization lies with the preachers, both male and female, and both clergy and non-clergy.

TRAINING YOUR TIMOTHY

Thus, the training and sending of preachers is probably one of the most critical ministries the body of Christ faces today. I believe that three important persons get involved and play a significant role to help shape a godly character in making a preacher: (1) God, (2), the mentor, and (3) the one being discipled. I would like to draw your attention first to the role of the mentor. Many scholars and Christian leaders came up with various definitions of the Great Commission in church history. While I'm aware that there're also several scriptures pointing to the Great Commission, such as Matthew 28:16–20; Mark 16:14–18; Luke 24:44–49; Acts 1:4–8; and John 20:19–23, I'll be mostly expounding on the most familiar fixture depicted by Matthew: "... Make disciples of *all nations* ..." The Great Commission stands out in its emphasis on discipling others across cultures and borders. If you are put to the position of the mentor to somebody, or if you wish to disciple somebody as your "Timothy," either on the mission field or at home, this section is for you.

Choosing Your Timothy

> Jesus went up on a mountainside and called to him those he wanted, and they came to him. He appointed twelve—designating them apostles. (Mark 3:13–14)

This text informs us that your Timothy should be recruited and trained in the church, in the way Jesus called his apostles on a mountainside: the word "mountain" in the Bible often symbolizes the church (Micah 4:1). Keep in mind that in most cases God has your Timothy *in* your church!

Notice that Jesus called them on a mountainside, not on a mountaintop. It means that your Timothy often could be found among those unrecognized in your church. Do not only look at the qualifications that may appear at the surface when choosing your Timothy. Try to look for his potential. Look at who God can make him into instead of who he is today. Envisioning his future will help you make the right choice. Remember that God chose David, the least among the sons of Jesse, to succeed King Saul and make his name and glory known to the nations.

It is fascinating that in the Bible it is always the teachers who chose the students, contrary to the common sense of the world today. Today, students search and choose the schools to go and teachers to sit under for their training. But, keep in mind that it was Moses who chose Joshua in the Bible. It was Elijah who chose Elisha. Also, Jesus himself chose his apostles, who would become his successors for the work of his kingdom. It is the mentor who must pray for and choose his God-given Timothy. Be sure to take time in much prayer before choosing your Timothy, as the Lord Jesus showed us an example in Luke 6:12–13 before choosing his apostles.

Training Your Timothy

I'm well aware that there are a great many curricula and teaching plans around us as for training our Timothy and successors in ministry. Carefully choose the ones that can work for your ministry style, leadership style, and spiritual gifts, etc. Keep nurturing your Timothy with God's Word.

Provide necessary correction, rebuke, and encouragement, along with great patience and careful instruction (2 Timothy 4:2). Continue to love him at all times—even when he may discourage you. And, remember that the greatest Timothy training method is *the example of your life*.

You should keep in mind that your Timothy does not belong to you, after all. You should not try to train him to be *your* man. If so, you will be tempted not to shape God's character in him but your own. Lead him to grow to full maturity in the Lord. Such an attitude does not start with the training methods but with your heart's desire of being a servant.

In addition, have a fatherly heart. A teacher can be jealous of his student's greater success, but a true mentor would be happy to see his Timothy reach a higher mark in ministry—even higher than his own. A father would not ask his own son to accomplish less than what he achieved. Rather, he would gladly sacrifice to pour out all his insights and know-how into his son, so that he may achieve even more.

If every senior leader would embrace such a heart in dealing with their assistants, the body of Christ would experience explosive growth. Jesus did not feel jealous about his disciples doing greater works than him (John 14:12). Let us remember the example of our Lord, who sacrificed himself on behalf of his disciples, including us, so that millions may be included in the kingdom today.

Treating Your Timothy

A mentor should value his Timothy. Cover your young Timothy's many mistakes. I admit that if it weren't for my mentor, the late Rev. Edward Park's cover-ups and patience, I would not have become who I am today. We can see that when the apostle Paul dealt with his disciples with his work-oriented personality until his regrettable confession at the end of his life (2 Timothy 4:11), nobody, including Timothy, was there for Paul during his imprisonment.

> ... Get Mark and bring him with you, because he is helpful to me in my ministry.

We read that it was Paul who rejected an idea of taking again young Mark, who did not show enduring faithfulness in his first missionary journey; Paul decided to go with Silas after a great dispute with Barnabas (Acts 15:36–41). It seems that Paul valued the achievement of his work more than his *people* during the earlier days of his ministry. We can learn this priceless lesson before the later days of our life: God values people more than works! Value your Timothy.

However, it is advisable to remain the same distance from all the Timothys around you instead of being close to a particular one. (Obviously, your Timothy does not have to be one only.) Also, you should not depend on your Timothy to the point that without him certain works in your ministry would not get done. Sow into the lives of as many people as you can. Expect God to bring about the harvest from those who have received it on the good soil of their hearts (Luke 8:8). In my experience as a mentor to preachers, I've seen those I least expected often surprisingly turn out to be the most fruitful ministers of the gospel. Sow your seeds widely. Then, God will reap the harvest in the end. In Christian discipleship, we may not exactly know who will be used by God and who won't be. This is because we can't fully figure out the person's heart. Only God can. Therefore, it is our solemn responsibility to sow the seeds of nurture and mentoring to everyone whom God brings on our path.

Passing on the Baton

Succession is a critical stage—perhaps the most important stage in your ministry—because it will measure the true impact you have laid there. Nevertheless, I have seen many strong churches and ministries get weaker—often even to the point of a split—after the succession. If your ministry experiences either stagnancy or diminishment after the succession, you probably need to examine your planning and "ownership." If the work truly is the Lord's, and you have so managed it, it should not only go on but produce even greater results after the ministry is handed over to your successor.

There are too many speaking about "*my* ministry" today. We should keep reminding ourselves that we are called to be the Lord's *servants*. A servant does not have anything that can be claimed as his own possession, even after years of works of service for his master. Praise from his master shall be the servant's only satisfaction. So it is with the Lord's servant. All the works of ministry belong to the Lord Jesus alone. He has graciously decided to share some of his works with his servants. We have been called to serve our portion of works in our times. There is no such thing as my own ministry. The work that you do will return to the Lord for accounting as soon as your time and portion are due. My ministries will not last beyond my death. But the Lord's ministry will have an impact even beyond my time, to eternity!

It has been said that a man is not successful until he is successfully succeeded by his successor. This was a burden God put in my heart when I went to Kenya as a missionary in 1996. During my days of leadership at EAPTC Africa, Eunice and I endeavored to commit ourselves to develop and mentor a team of national leaders with the intention of eventually turning over the ministry to them. We believed that it was the only way to consistent growth of the schools and churches. The signs we looked for in timing our succession were four things: (1) confirmation both in personal and corporate prayers, (2) change of the circumstances leading to the need for national leadership, (3) proof of maturity in the national leadership, and (4) commitment to self-support, self-governing, and self-propagation within the ministry. In our case, God had met those conditions by the end of 2011. Then, Eunice and I believed it was time. We've felt that the ministry has been enhanced, not weakened, after the transition.

In choosing your successor, please do not consider how your successor may treat you later on. Yes, it will be proper for your successor to treat his previous leader with care and respect, knowing that someday he will also need to pass on the ministry to someone else, but that should not be the main factor in choosing your successor. Let the Lord choose and arrange the man after his own heart (1 Samuel 13:14). Trust God to reveal the right person and the right time.

Lastly, commit your successor unto the safe hand of our Lord and the power of his Word, as the apostle Paul did with the elders of the church from Ephesus in Acts 20:31. Even after the succession, be sure to give your full support to your successor by *praying* for him to make the right decisions at every turn of the ministry. Do not fall into the temptation of continuing to *tell* him what to do or how to do about every issue. Remember that the Lord is very able to continue to build his own body without you. Do your best to help your successor firmly establish his roots in the new ministry.

MULTIPLYING CROSS-CULTURALLY

Given the fact that 95 percent of pastors in the world are untrained,[1] I saw the critical need in this area when I began my first career missionary service in Kenya. This is the story of how God has worked in Africa and even Asia through those who responded to the need of society and call of God.

After my cross-cultural experience over decades in three different continents, my research on what makes cross-cultural discipleship successful stretched further. It has convinced me, at least, that cross-cultural

---

1. Richard, "Training of Pastors."

discipleship should focus more on people than any other issue. Charles Kraft pointed it out when he wrote, "As cross-cultural workers, our aim is first to understand the *people* to whom we go."[2] Again, the Great Commission is about making disciples of different nations by reaching out to them. Disciple-making is an integral part of any type of missionary work. To this end, I came to discover that a cross-cultural disciple-maker should consider the following three factors in his attempt to carry out this imperative task. Discipleship is *not* primarily about programs but the imitation of the mentor. A mentor's exemplary lifestyle in the following three rules is fundamental for the effective multiplication of discipleship.

1. Incarnational Ministry of the Mentor

Tireless efforts should be made by fishers of men to get *into* their fish pool and to become one of the "fish" for most effective fishing. A process of incarnation is vitally important. The gospel can be effectively delivered only when a missionary understands his people and the world in which they live. The Son of God became the son of man that the sons of men might become the sons of God. The word "incarnation" comes from the Latin word *in-carne* (*in-* + *carō*), which means "flesh" or "a voluntary act of assuming flesh." The incarnational ministry of a missionary mentor is of absolute necessity. Moreover, it was my verdict that most of the successful missionaries in cross-cultural discipleship witnessed three common points in their mentoring efforts.

First, a missionary mentor should experience the incarnation in his perception of local concepts. This is not about whether to refuse or accept or to criticize or support local concepts; it is about simply understanding them, often the root of such concepts. Such efforts build a bridge of relationship that usually leads to witness of Christ. One's missionary work must be built on a long-term perspective, as if he's running a marathon. This long race ought to begin with a proper understanding of local concepts. Nearsighted, hasty, and judgmental criticism can only damage his ministry of disciple-making. No matter how retrogressive a civilization one's mission field is, if missionaries try hard enough, they can certainly uncover some good things within that particular culture. They can actually learn to respect those cultural treasures upon finding them. By doing so, a missionary experiences stepping closer toward becoming one with the very people he went to serve.

Second, a missionary's life, both in public and in private, ought to enjoy a rich volume of interpersonal relationships with various types of people, both

---

2. Kraft, *Anthropology for Christian Witness*, 10. Emphasis added.

local people and other missionaries. He should not have "enemies." Well-socialized interpersonal relationships seemed a vivid sign of all successful missionary mentors I've met. They're blessers, not cursers, under any circumstance. Most of them are even familiar with the "norm" of betrayals in their ministry to people; they seem to have grasped the meaning of Richard Bach's old saying, "If you love someone, set them free. If they come back they're yours; if they don't they never were." All successful missionary mentors try to sustain healthy relationships with *everyone* around them.

Third, a missionary mentor should make an effort to adapt to live with the local economy and living standard of his mission field. This is rather a serious challenge for some missionaries who originated from the First World and find their mission fields in the less developed Two-Thirds World[3] countries. It is a matter of how humble-hearted missionaries should live on the mission field, not of how much they should live with. Humility will help missionary mentors learn to minimize their living expenses and to narrow any unnecessary economy gaps between local disciples and themselves. Jesus never showed his superiority to the people he was serving, although he came from heaven where everything was far better than earth. He became one of the Jews. Jesus humbly accepted even the limitation of flesh and blood. Prolific cross-cultural disciple-makers do not complain about the low standard of life that often exists on the mission field. Romans 1:1–2 teaches us to offer our bodies as living sacrifices every day. Life on the mission field can be a good opportunity to practice this timeless teaching. Missionary mentors should *never* assert the superiority of their national origins on the mission field. We'll discuss incarnation and cultural homogenization issues more in chapter 10.

2. Ministry Foundation of the One Being Discipled

The parable of the sower in Matthew 13:3–9 exemplifies four different kinds of ministry foundations of gospel workers. The same text defines those foundations as "soils." A farmer (representing the Lord) goes out to sow his seed (representing the Word, see verses 18–23). All of God's works begin with the Word, and the instructions of God's Word and teachable ears (see verse 9) to take heed of them is another crucial factor in making genuine disciples in a cross-cultural environment. A disciple without the foundation of the word of encouragement and exhortation may deteriorate to the first three categories: seeds fallen along the path (no decency), or on

---

3. In this book, the terms like "Two-Thirds World," "Majority World" and "Global South" are interchangeably used.

rocky places (no maturity), or among thorns (no wholesomeness). Local disciples nurtured well in exemplary teachings of the Word will produce other disciples who are likewise grounded on good soil in the long run.

I happened to discover in my research that the ministry foundation of the one being discipled matters a great deal in cross-cultural discipleship. The following research was done with two Kenyan pastors whom I have personally trained and worked with in our mission in past years. By comparing the following two cases, I wish to exhibit how one's ministry foundation affects his path of discipleship. For the sake of privacy, I have used their initials for this presentation.

Case #1 (Success Case)—Church I and Pastor EO

EO was called to ministry while he was still a high school teacher by profession. By then, he was wholeheartedly serving as a deacon in one of our local churches in western Kenya. It was obvious that Deacon EO was then being equipped for his future ministry through church life. EO's lifestyle was exemplary in many ways: he was a devoted tither, a faithful deacon, and a Sunday school teacher. He was altogether obedient and supportive to his leaders in the church. He was praised by the majority of his churchmates.

Toward the end of his Bible school training, EO was licensed as a pastor by our mission and planted a church in his hometown. The beginning of his church planting experience wasn't easy for him at all. Some people in his hometown showed reluctance to join his church. Some did not even approve of him as genuinely called by God, while others simply ignored what he was doing. Only with a handful of people, he and his wife started a home cell meeting in his house in 1999. He faithfully nourished his few members and fostered a spirit of unity among them by patiently proving to them the sincerity of his call. As the cell group that he started in his house grew bigger in number, a new cell naturally emerged out of the first cell. Soon, from those two cells four other cells emerged, and it went on with more multiplication. The cell members were learning to encourage one another and getting passionate about giving birth to more new cells. In the process, the members were being equipped by church life, and the small group meetings became a life-giving resource to them. Also, knowing the power of teaching as an educator himself, especially that of the Bible teaching, Pastor EO put much emphasis on equipping his church members through the teaching of the Word and a balanced church life. He made sure that everything he taught came from the Bible: giving, prayer, baptism, Communion, etc. He began to teach his people about the A-to-Z of Christian life, faith, and church life, without any extortion or coercion. Instead, Pastor EO kept believing in the power of God's Word to convince and change people.

Such a church planting approach as EO's wasn't, and still isn't, very popular in Africa. In many African churches, Bible teaching is not the major emphasis of ministry; they'd rather heavily depend on miracles, music, and even politics. Several youths left the church and joined other churches where they felt the worship style was more "attractive." Nevertheless, his disciple-making efforts paid off, and in the third year of his ministry the church celebrated an installment of eight deacons. All those eight believers were led to Christ by Pastor EO himself three years earlier. Church I, however, still marked around forty people in its total membership by this time.

Then, Pastor EO put those eight leaders into work and had them lead different departments of the church, from Sunday school to choir. He also introduced overnight prayer meetings to his church so that anyone with needs could come and pray in the church. Pastor EO turned Church I into a praying church. He made sure that someone prays in the church 365 days a year. People who had tasted the blessings of prayer volunteered to fill in the gaps so that the chain of daily prayers would not get broken. As time went by, more and more people got equipped by coming to Jesus every day.

EO's case may well be a marvelous example of a pastor whose life and church ministry hasn't been moved by the necessities but by the Holy Spirit. He was not anxious about church growth or leadership installment. He developed a habit of waiting upon the Holy Spirit to open a door and even pave tangible ways before making important decisions or attempting any project in the church. Pastor EO became known as a man of great character as a result.

In a little over ten years, Church I grew to four hundred people in Sunday attendance, had thirty-eight cell groups within the church, and planted five other daughter congregations. In 2010, Pastor EO was elected to be a national overseer of Kenya churches in our mission, which comprised around forty congregations nationwide by then. Church I and Pastor EO's life and ministry are a classic example of how God can equip anyone willing to ground himself on the good soil of the teachings of his Word through longsuffering. He knew the power of the Word to bring up himself and others.

Case #2 (Failure Case)—Church II and Pastor SI

SI grew up in a slum in Kenya. He joined our Church II congregation years ago and soon found favor in the eyes of the church leadership back then.

He seemed faithful over the next few years, participating in most of the church activities. SI became a deacon after a while, despite that he had been in the church for a considerably shorter time than other leaders. A time came when the pastor of Church II resigned and abruptly had to leave Kenya. Leaders of Church II contacted us at the central mission office and asked for another pastor. The mission introduced several candidates to the church; however, the members didn't feel content with them coming from outside of their community. Having tarried several months without a pastor, the mission and church agreed that the members would choose a pastor among themselves. With around 60 percent votes, a young, charismatic SI who had just finished his Bible school training was elected to be their new pastor despite his short history in the church. In other words, SI did not have enough time to get equipped in church life before he became a pastor, yet he was the congregation's ultimate choice then.

As soon as SI became a pastor, conflicts arose between him and the existing church leadership. One by one, the existing leaders left, beginning with the church treasurer. SI's wife quickly replaced the treasurer's position. All the influential and "front-seat" roles in the church were refilled by his family members and relatives. Besides, since SI took over the church, the Bible study meetings were rarely held in the church. Chances of the flock being fed and equipped by God's Word remarkably decreased. Instead, SI's preaching ministry heavily emphasized on giving, the prosperity gospel, and healings. Particularly the old members of the church left for other churches, one by one. The rest, who were not familiar with the church's history, kept the church moving. However, when they got acquainted with the inside story, a number of them left as well sooner or later. But scores of new youths kept joining Church II due to Pastor SI's flamboyant leadership style. And this cycle of old members' departure and new members' arrival routinely continued for years.

The major blow to Church II came when SI announced a fundraising drive for church construction. Most of his church members with spiritual malnutrition did not yield to his appeal to give toward construction. Instead of calling for prayer meetings for God to meet the particular need of the church, a frustrated Pastor SI rather turned his eyes on prospective rich donors from abroad. Knowing that their pastor was no longer interested in their small, sacrificial giving, even a minority of faithful givers in the church stopped giving toward the project. At this point, Pastor SI became even more interested in motivating his foreign donors than feeding his church members. No church initiatives for their own fundraising efforts were necessary in this regard. Both SI and his church members lost touch with God at this stage. God was no longer their source of blessing. There was hardly any equipping of saints or making of disciples. Besides, having tasted once or twice some large amount of donations from abroad, SI didn't even find a reason to respect his spiritual authority, let alone his church elders, whom he wanted to put under his control all along. Waiting upon and being equipped by the Holy Spirit was no longer Pastor SI's way of doing the things in ministry. Impressing foreign donors by all means to get the funds he desires grew to be his major concern.

Over a period of time, the donors who gave generously out of their compassion for the poor of an African slum found out that their donations toward Church II had not been used as designated. It was later discovered that most of the contributions directly went into Pastor SI's personal account. Furious donors dropped out and moved away with their supports. Pastor SI, who became desperate with no donors remaining with him, began to relate to a cult-related organization that promised him a large sum of donations should he cooperate with them. Spiritual issues were no longer SI's interest. Getting money out of some rich foreign donors in the name of "church business" turned out to be his way of survival. When Pastor SI became aware that he was in danger of excommunication from our mission by joining a cult, he even persuaded members of Church II that his authorities in the mission were trying to divide his church on a tribal basis. At the deception of Pastor SI's persuasive gestures, Church II left our mission and formed their own mission years ago. Church II and Pastor SI's case is an example of how one can lead himself and others downhill when he refuses to build his life and ministry on the good soil of the Word and its disciplines. SI's insufficient amount of preparation and his opportunistic slum mentality contributed to his ministry being rooted in other unsteady foundations.

These two case studies reflect that the upright ministry foundation of the Word and teachable ears can make a significant difference in discipleship training of the one being discipled. Even though an equal training opportunity may be given to all, only the ones with a fit foundation must excel in the end. Hence, it is a missionary mentor's obligation on the mission field to pray for God's blessings and wisdom to find and discern those with good soil.

3. Effective Administrative System for Indigenous Expansions

Cross-cultural disciple-makers may need to explore Christ's strategy on world evangelization deeper. Jesus, a missionary from heaven, took the initiative of discipling just a handful of local apprentices as he envisioned the rest of the world coming to him. The apostle Paul planted mother churches in urban areas through which he saw other daughter congregations budding off in the surroundings, as we see this principle from Acts 16:9–12 and 2 Timothy 2:2. If properly nurtured and well guided, mother churches established in urban settings naturally grow with loaded access and resources to plant daughter churches in other *ethnos* (tribes).[4] It has been the mechanism of the church planting movement (CPM), a rapid and multiplicative increase of indigenous churches planting churches within a given people group or population segment, formerly affirmed by David Garrison of the Southern Baptist Convention.[5] My research confirms that an effective administration for natural, indigenous expansion is needed for multiplicative cross-cultural discipleship. We've seen in our ministry that cross-cultural discipling effort is promoted when it is backed by a sensible administration for free and indigenous expansion.

Like many other missionaries in their first terms, my early years of missionary work in Kenya had a series of disappointments and discouragements. My greatest struggle among a dozen other ones was to identify a practical methodology of cross-cultural discipleship. After experiencing some frustrating results in church planting and cross-cultural mission while working with a traditional Bible school in Nairobi, we changed to the discipleship-based Bible training center by adopting a lesson plan from DCI Global Partnerships of England at the beginning of my second missionary term. This new strategy has assisted us to challenge our churches to plant daughter churches by training their key church leaders. Since then, our graduates have opened nearly three hundred new churches and Bible training centers in Kenya, Uganda, Tanzania, Burundi, South Sudan, DR Congo, Malawi, Zambia, Mozambique, Zimbabwe, South Africa, South Korea, China, and Vietnam (as of 2019). A survey in 2010 of over one thousand graduates of our Bible training centers showed that 70 percent of them were serving in full-time or part-time ministry, 20 percent of them planted new churches of various denominational backgrounds, 5 percent of them planted new churches under our mission's church umbrella, and 3 percent of them were running daughter Bible training centers with our mission (see Figure 1). Some of those churches and training centers that multiplied into different African states have begun orphanages, kindergartens, literature productions, micro-finance banking projects, and radio broadcasts on their own for community transformation.

---

4. For related discussions on this topic, see "Why Plant Churches?," http://download.redeemer.com/pdf/learn/resources/Why_Plant_Churches-Keller.pdf.

5. See Garrison *Church Planting Movements*.

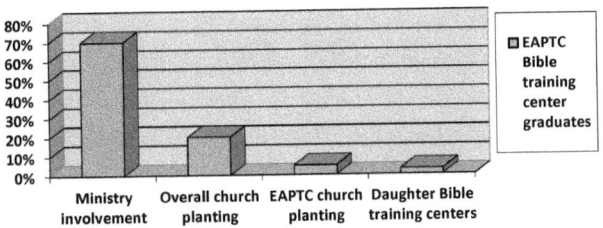

Figure 1. EAPTC mission evaluation, 2010

Regarding the multiplicative expansion of our mission, an observer once said, "EAPTC Bible training center is... opening more churches and schools of their own, mothers, daughters and grand-daughters" (see Figure 2).

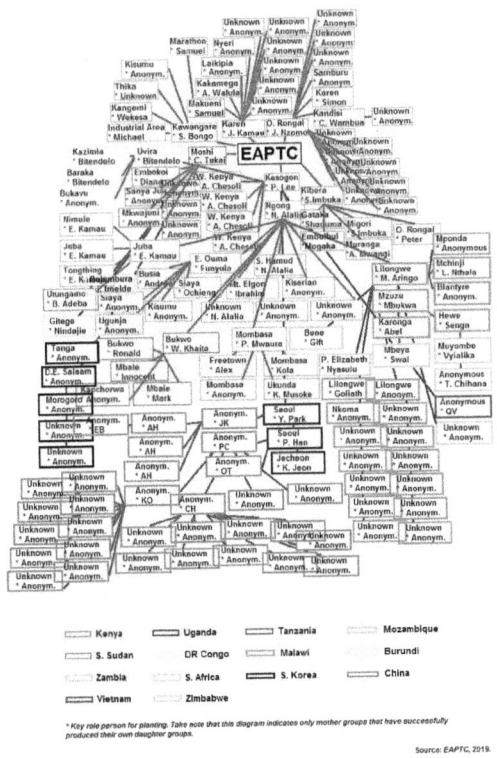

Figure 2. Family tree of EAPTC churches and schools, 2019[6]

6. This multiplication family tree of EAPTC was originally drawn out by Pastor Hamon Kim, who visited Africa with us six times in past, and it was later modified in

EAPTC's mission has been expanding through its unique multiplication methodology of cross-cultural discipleship. It shows how God has been blessing the work for years through the biblical multiplication of discipleship and church planting.

Since 2002, EAPTC Bible training centers worldwide have been operating and expanding through self-multiplication in the following pattern:

1. Applications are taken for the next course.

2. A prayerful selection procedure of eight to fifteen students per course takes place.

3. The discipleship training program is offered part-time or full-time, in any available room, no expensive special facilities needed. The atmosphere is outward-looking to unreached people groups and the nations, and the expectancy is that many students will go and open a new school elsewhere, form a new church around it, or at the very least return to their home churches as better equipped men and women to serve with the pastor.

Picture 1. First Bible training center graduation, Nairobi, 2004

2009 into a handy format. It has been updated with the portion of Asian expansion later in 2019.

4. A graduation ceremony is held. Willing and qualified graduates get official authorizations to repeat the course in other locations. The graduates become the teachers, and a copy of the school curriculum is made available for purchase at a minimal cost. No expensive materials or unaffordable technologies are needed to take the training elsewhere.

Picture 2. Second Bible training center graduation, Nairobi, 2004

5. The graduates return to their home churches. The home church becomes a mother church by sending out the graduate to repeat the Bible training center in another urban or rural community, or even over the border in another country.

Picture 3. Daughter Bible training center over the border in Malawi, 2006

6. The same process then repeats. The new indigenous Bible training center is advertised by word of mouth, applications are taken, and eight to fifteen students are prayerfully selected. The new school repeats the same program part-time or full-time. The graduate has become the director/teacher/pastor by this stage. The uncomplicated training leads to prayers, outreaches, worship, and fellowship. This is by and large consolidated into a daughter church, which is financially supported by the mother church.

Picture 4. Granddaughter congregation in Zambia, 2010

7. Meanwhile, the mother Bible training center and other existing training schools hold another course and repeat the same process from the first step.[7]

SIMILAR KIND, LESS FRICTION

I came to believe that whatever type of work a missionary may be involved in in the field, his disciple-making effort must be duplicated and multiplied. It lies at the very heart of the Great Commission: "... teaching them to *obey* everything I have commanded you ..." (Matthew 28:20). It was my observation that this multiplicative system requires missionaries to abide in three major principles to effectively produce disciples in a cycle. Above all, a missionary has to be localized. Only then can the missionary could produce sound local leaders. This then results in the produced local leaders converting and guiding other local people. Such a system provided us advantages for not making unnecessary mistakes in dealing with unfamiliar cultures on the mission field, and in the process also taught us a principle of, what I call, "similar kind, less friction." Over the years in my disciple-making efforts with Kenyan church leaders, I found that *a similar kind causes less friction* in every area of life, including the cross-cultural ministry.

Oftentimes, I had to encounter situations whereby I had to challenge some ungodly practices that do exist in African cultures. I confronted them again and again, yet the response was considerably low in turnout. Later on, I happened to notice that when the same challenge was given by one of my disciples who originated from the same tribal background as those practicing the unsound rituals, his remarks were taken more seriously and eventually helped them replace such rituals with alternative godly practices. I experienced similar cases time and time again to prove this principle to be more likely universal. Simply speaking, homogeneity causes less friction when confronting local people, yet it reaches deeper in them with apparent influence.

7. For more information, see "How Does the School of Mission Work Best?," https://dci.org.uk/how-does-school-work-best.

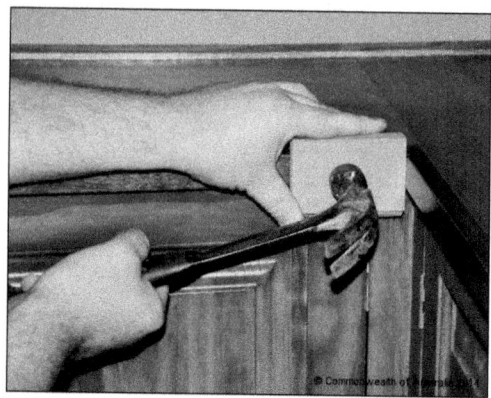

Similarly, all skillful carpenters would know how not to leave ugly hammer marks on timbers when they're nailing. When a nail is almost inserted in the timber, they place a piece of timber on the top of the nail and hammer on that timber instead of hitting directly on the nail. A carpenter knows that another timber absorbs the shock and therefore it does not leave a mark. Our Lord Jesus, once a carpenter himself while on earth, knew this and probably wanted to teach us the same principle to be more prudent witnesses to the ends of the earth.

This fascinating principle leads us to another significant reason why a missionary *must* make disciples in whatever type of work he may do on the field. Seasoned disciples who are made among the local people often can and *will* penetrate their own cultures and change the lives and communities with the message more effectively than missionaries. After all, a missionary should expect to see God's glory through the maturity and success of his disciples. No wonder Jesus, the greatest missionary of all times, gave this peerless mission strategy to his body that follows in his footsteps: "... make *disciples* of all *nations* ..." He knew what he was talking about.

MULTIPLICATIVE NATURE OF BIBLICAL DISCIPLESHIP

The Old Testament is about the perversion and preservation of God's will, plan, and message while the New Testament is about the provision and propagation of the same. For the methodology of that propagation, God chose a channel of discipleship. The discipleship model of Jesus and 2 Timothy 2:2—"And the things you have heard me say in the presence of many witnesses entrust to reliable men who will also be qualified to teach others"—visibly demonstrate that a biblical chain of discipleship progresses in the following prototype.

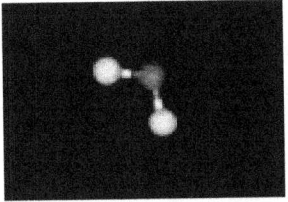

Picture 5. Multiplication stage 1

The mother church and several small daughters are represented in this picture. A missionary mentor teaches a group of local leaders, and one or two of them takes and duplicates the same propaganda elsewhere.

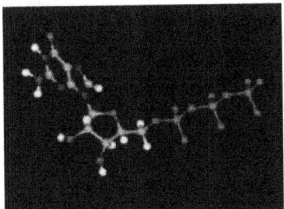

Picture 6. Multiplication stage 2

The above picture illustrates where we were after a decade of work in Africa. The mother church is still active and is cooperated with at this point by many growing interdependent hubs, most of whom have their own daughter churches, schools, and projects. Many of our students were, and are, under the mentorship of local leaders who are graduates of the earlier trainings given by missionaries.

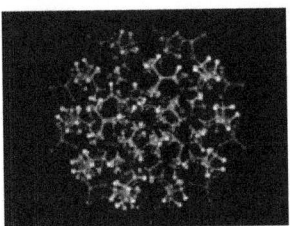

Picture 7. Multiplication stage 3

This is the stage we're moving into. It is what we have been envisioning from the very beginning—a network of churches and training schools covering Africa and Asia and the nations. There will not be just one central point giving life to the rest or controlling all, but a network of interdependent hubs each linked to Christ and loosely to one another, each giving births to its new daughters, which in turn give birth to their granddaughters.[8] In case any link fails, the network will still recover and continue to move onward. Thanks to this biblical administrative system for indigenous expansion, our work in Africa and Asia is targeting to open ten thousand new churches and Bible training schools in various regions of the world, and we trust we are well on the way by God's grace.

> From him the whole body, joined and held together by every supporting ligament, grows and builds itself up in love, as each part does its work. (Ephesians 4:16)

There is something the body of Christ can learn from the marketing strategy of the Coca-Cola Company. Coca-Cola is one of the most propagated brands in the world today.[9] Their careful research, powerful strategy, and amazing motivation put them at the top of the chart among their competitors. I have noticed that Coca-Cola is so flexible with their product names, as long as they're getting sold, but is extremely cautious to preserve their formula. Many do not even know that beverages like Sprite, Fanta, Dasani, Minute Maid, and more are owned by the Coca-Cola Company.

Just as Coca-Cola introduced various product names that contextually connected with local needs when they entered new countries for business, EAPTC decided years ago to give freedom to national leadership to create their own church names at the onset of entering new mission fields. Besides, this strategy has been affirmed as one of the characteristics of the twenty-first-century independent churches that have sprung up in almost every continent, following the current move of the Holy Spirit. Generally, they're not apt to foreign control or missionary control. Sometimes, new wines should be put into new wineskins. EAPTC, on the other hand, has endeavored to improve on every possible weakness of indigenous national churches, including disunity and exposure to heretical teachings, by persistently emphasizing the importance of teamwork and constant Bible teaching. It wasn't easy at times, owing to rampant tribal conflicts in Africa and occasional exploitation of cult groups invading the continent

---

8. For related discussions on this topic, see "More Time with Les and Pilar," https://www.dci.org.uk/main/moretime.htm.

9. McKinnon and Cumbers, *Introduction to Economic Geography Globalization*, 83.

in the name of donations and aids for economical vulnerability. God kept us moving onward. National ministry boards have intentionally consisted of the elected leaders from various tribal and provincial backgrounds. Corporate meetings and personal coaching sessions for national leaders have been held on a periodical basis. Every training curricula has been standardized, shared, and closely monitored.

On top of the major axes of leadership training, church planting, and children's ministry, EAPTC presently operates additional ministries like film evangelism, nursery schools, literature production, micro-finance banking projects, radio broadcasts, and orphanages in some countries where it works. Over the years, indigenous local bodies of EAPTC have wrought out contextualized evangelistic efforts that suit the distinctive needs of locality and community. In the Creative Access Regions of Asia, leaders have come up with and ran more unconventional and secretive approaches to reach out to the tangible needs of their communities.

CROSSING BORDERS

Often, the same or similar language groups and cultures make habitants of two or three neighboring countries over the political boundaries. For example, Chilengo town in Central Africa connects the three countries of Malawi, Zambia, and Mozambique all in its neighborhood. Busia town connects and is composed of a polyglot population that spreads out both in Kenya and Uganda across the border. Such strategic areas are where we have found a key for cross-cultural penetration and international expansion of the gospel. We at EAPTC have discovered it to be quite effective to equip a Kenyan disciple in Busia and send him to the other side of Busia town, situated over in Uganda and even beyond toward inland within the neighboring country. In such towns, life is inexplicably intertwined and culturally melted. A person from those areas has rarely experienced cultural shocks and a deficiency in adaptability when he has been sent to serve over the border.

After all, people groups have existed long before the national borders known today. Countries of the modern day are not the "nations" the Bible talks about. For example, Africa existed as tribes and clans (the biblical definition of "nations") long before the European colonizers made national demarcations. That is what Jesus meant by "the nations." Even in the Bible, we read of regions that appear to have different names but they're simply the same old place. The names of countries and regions may change throughout history, depending on who conquers the land and who writes about it. However, the Bible, the everlasting Word of God, describes places mostly with their original names. Older than dirt, God knows their true identity.

Often, we who live in modern days can be distracted and even deceived to think the names in the ancient Bible have nothing to do with our daily life today. That is certainly not how our God, who transcends the time and space, views and orchestrates the history. For instance, Israel was called the land of Canaan before the Israelites arrived, and it was called Philistia (Psalm 60:8; 87:4; 108:9) later and Palestine after the Jewish Revolt. Iraq is frequently mentioned in the Bible, second only to Israel, but by other names like Ur, Babylon, Mesopotamia, and possibly Shinar, where the tower of Babel was erected. Egypt also appears under names like Elim, Kadesh-Barnea in the Bible records, and Kement in other ancient writings.[10]

Nevertheless, we should be careful to note that time and again God calls the places by their original identities. In the Bible, God frequently reminds people about who they are by calling them by their very original names. Egypt is indicated as the land of Ham in Psalm 105:23 and 27. Simply put, people determine the places. The Bible focuses more on people than places. So should our concept of biblical mission. Once we understand a people, we understand their place. This is why cross-cultural missionaries must be well acquainted with the history of people of the land they wish to reach.

---

10. Obenga, "Egypt: Ancient History of African Philosophy," 31.

MISSIONARY ANTHROPOLOGY

I incubated the entire African continent as one cluster, having come from a common Bible figure as the forefather—Ham. The Bible tells us that the history restarted with Noah and his three sons, after the destruction of the initial mankind by the flood. Their names were Shem, Ham, and Japheth.

> The sons of Noah who came out of the ark were Shem, Ham, and Japheth (Ham was the father of Canaan). These were the three sons of Noah, and "from them came the people who were scattered over the earth" (Genesis 9:18–19).

While there're no little anthropological controversy about the biblical lineage of ancestors, it is most commonly perceived that Ham is an ancestor of Africans and Palestinians while Japheth is that of Europeans, European settlers in the Americas, Oceania, Africa, and some of the Indians. Shem is likely to be an ancestor of Jews, some Arabs, and some Asians.[11] It is virtually untraceable to figure one's family tree with its detailed subsets after hundreds of generations of intertribal and interethnic marriages amid countless migration of people from one place to another. Yet, these three lineages of Shem, Ham, and Japheth undeniably tend to show cultural and behavioral distinctives in various dimensions.

From the biblical perspective, a principle of cultural formations assumes that:

1. All cultures are subsets of the biblical family tree of Shem, Ham, and Japheth. "These are the clans of Noah's sons, according to their lines of descent, within their nations. *From these the nations spread out over the earth* after the flood" (Genesis 10:32).

2. They were a family and siblings. Therefore, they lived together, at least in the beginning. "This is the account of *Shem, Ham and Japheth, Noah's sons, who themselves had sons* after the flood" (Genesis 10:1).

Genesis 10 suggests genealogical multiplications according to their lines of descent. They each formed lines of the Shemites, Hamites, and Japhethites and spread out over the earth. This record theoretically suggests to us that if a missionary biblically discovers his identification with the local people on the mission field and culturally finds homogenization with them, cross-cultural discipleship is likely to trace its theological root. Discipleship across cultures is quite feasible because mankind came from one family

---

11. Lee, *Missionary Candidate Training*, 26.

after all. It should be even more conversantly so with those in the same lineage or close lineage.

In a sense, EAPTC took this principle into its experimental fieldwork. Our experience attests firsthand to the theory that discipleship can naturally spread from one culture to another similar culture over the border. We've seen it working from Kenya to Uganda, Tanzania and Malawi, from Uganda to South Sudan, from Tanzania to Burundi and DR Congo, from Malawi to Zambia, Mozambique, Zimbabwe and South Africa, from South Korea to China and Philippines, and for the latest from the Philippines to Vietnam. Indeed, a similar kind can produce disciples cross-culturally with more relevancies and less frictions.

It implies that every man and woman on earth is a member of a huge family, forgotten over a vast time gap and geographical chasm. Also, it logically defies any racist attitude against one another including, but not limited to, tribalism, ethnic hatred, localism, and so on. Cross-cultural ministry begins with the biblical foundation and anthropological reflection that all men are sinners and are in dire need of Christ, the Savior. This provides the ultimate common ground for missionaries to reach out to the nations.

While ministering in Asia, Africa, and America, I have observed different methodologies being applied by effective communicators and vision-casters to motivate people. A channel of motivation is experimentally different in these three said cultures.

- In African culture, it should be focused on the common initiator.
- In European/American culture, it should be focused on the common interest.
- In Asian culture, it should be focused on the common ideology.

Research by the Lausanne Movement supports the idea that even the world's cultural zones are characterized into three categories. They're namely: (1) honor-shame cultural zone, (2) power-fear cultural zone, and (3) innocence-guilt cultural zone.

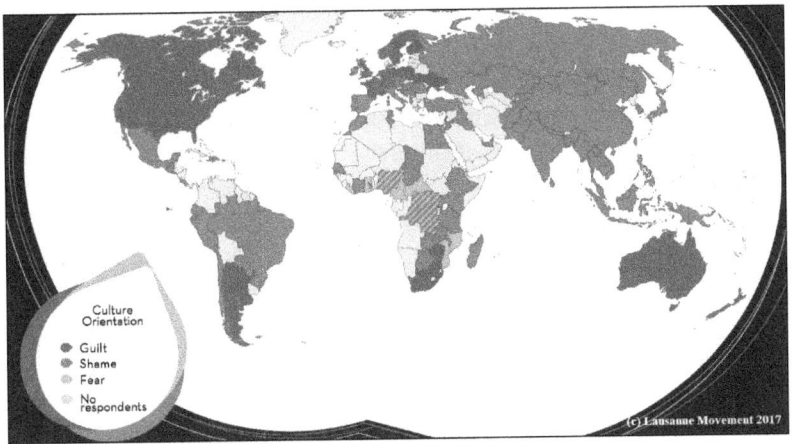

Concerning the biblical exercise of disciplinary actions for cross-cultural discipleship, cross-cultural missionaries must keep in mind which cultural zone their ministry falls under. Void of such valuable knowledge, a missionary may damage the long-established relationship with local disciples at the expense of the unintentional creation of shame or fear or guilt in their minds. To give an illustration, when I was ministering in the Far East, characterized as a Semitic cultural zone with the concept of saving face, I learned I should never rebuke a leader to impose shame on him in front of others unless public confession is vividly at hand.

Our experience convincingly shows that it was more conversant for Africans to reach Africa, Asians to reach Asia, and Europeans (and European settlers in the Americas and Oceania) to reach Europe (and European settlers in the Americas and Oceania). It would make a natural sense, considering the many similarities that exist within the three big cultural lineages of Shem, Ham, and Japheth. During my frequent ministry travels across Africa and Asia to go visit my disciples and their churches, the Lord repeatedly pounded this biblical implication into my soul: *Africa shall be best reached by Africans, Asia by Asians, and Europe and America by Europeans and Americans.*

Then I theorized that it would be culturally less hassling for people of the same biblical lineage to cross cultures within the same lineage. Most of Africa falls under a cultural lineage of Ham and his descendants. Hence, this principle was put into practice and has worked smoothly for tribes near the national borders to cross from one culture to other neighboring cultures. Our work has mostly spread along Anglophone regions of the African continent. It initially blossomed in Kenya and went over the border to Uganda through a Kenyan missionary we dispatched. English and

Kiswahili were the languages through which he communicated the message with Ugandans. The next missionary was sent from Kenya to South Sudan, another English-speaking nation on the top of Arabic and local vernaculars. Tanzania, another neighboring country to Kenya, soon came into our radar. Kenyans are au fait at communicating the message in English and Kiswahili. A Kenyan pastor, a native of the Maasai tribe, was selected and trained to be our next missionary to Tanzania. Again, the Maasai tribe has its presence both in Kenya and Tanzania, spreading over their bordering line. He was easily accepted by his clan on the Tanzanian side and began his ministry soon upon arrival in Kilimanjaro/Moshi area in 2003. His life and mission work continues to bear amazing fruit of cross-tribal discipleship and church planting across major towns of Tanzania and other Swahili-speaking countries of Africa.

Our Kenyan missionaries and their works were as effective as other missionaries from the non-African background were, but fewer hassles were involved in the process of cultural adaptation. Not only that, but it also took a shorter amount of time for them to adjust to new community life, which could've taken years for missionaries from non-African backgrounds to do. Due to European colonial history, most Africans possess a gift of the ability to speak other languages. Though it has left a severe scar, God has turned their mourning into dancing and is using their multilinguistic ability to share his message to the nations.

Just as the early expansion of the gospel paralleled the ancient commercial route of the Silk Road, our initial work in Africa expanded mostly following the Common Market for Eastern and Southern Africa countries, commonly known as COMESA. Christ's disciples were raised and God's churches planted on the COMESA line. Following Paul's strategic example, our mission would prayerfully target developing suburban towns with intentional planting of the mother church in mind. Regularly benefitted by the economy flux in COMESA, many people sought to migrate in and out of those towns, and it turned out to be quite strategic in a long run because those job-seekers and business-traders spread the flames of discipleship over cultural and national borders after they were discipled by us. Many of our disciples were people "on the move" and God's movement was sparked up. Countless lives have been changed for eternity by the movement. Though unseen, the vision was incubated in me and my team. It was a matter of time for it to be birthed into reality.

In Asia, missionaries sent by EAPTC Korea and EAPTC China continue to faithfully reach out to other Asian nations. Some of them train the house church leaders while others plant local churches in East Asian countries. Some help run a music ministry and orphanage in the Philippines. The rising popularity of Korean pop (K-pop) culture and the economic growth of China have paved the way for Koreans and Chinese to take the gospel and shine the light of Christ in other regions of Asia. Asia is being reached by Asians. This validates the reason our Lord Jesus instructed us to make disciples of all "nations" (ἔθνη or *ethne* in Greek), which literally means the people group, language group, or ethnicity. My team at EAPTC put that wisdom into practice and has been seeing the outcome over decades. Neighboring cultures, tribes, and clans have easier access to cross a border to others around. This flame of cross-cultural discipleship has no limit to spread over national or cultural barriers should we abide in this biblical principle.

DISCUSSION AND REFLECTION QUESTIONS

1. Lee states that your Timothy may be found among those unrecognized around you just as Jesus called his disciples on a mountainside, not on a mountaintop. The person may look insignificant at the moment, but God may envision a great leader in him and wants to use you to mold him. Do you have someone God is leading you to reach out and help mature in faith?

2. Matthew 13:3-8, 18-23 elaborates on four kinds of ministry foundations of the person being discipled. How would you describe the person whose ministry foundation is grounded on the good soil in Jesus' parable?

3. Jesus commanded his body to make disciples of all "nations" (ἔθνη or *ethne* in Greek), which literally means the people group, language group, or ethnicity. Discuss why it is important that every missionary work revolves on cross-cultural discipleship as the earth revolves on its axis.

6

The Holy Spirit, Mastermind of World Mission

THE HOLY SPIRIT FOR WORLD MISSION

> Leave your country, your people and your father's household and go to the land I will show you. I will make you into a great nation and I will bless you. I will make your name great, and you will be a blessing. I will bless those who bless you, and whoever curses you I will curse; *and all peoples on earth will be blessed through you.* (Genesis 12:1–3)

Christians need to align their life-view with God's will and the biblical purpose of believers on earth. I believe the Abrahamic blessing in Genesis 12:1–3 is a foremost missional mandate to which all born-again believers of all walks and careers should strive to contribute in this one life given. Blessing the world with our God-given blessings ought to be our highest priority. It should be stamped as our worldview and life-view.

In Acts 2, multiple *nations* were represented on the Pentecost and orchestrated by God to witness the birth of the Church. Before that in Acts 1:8, the missional mandate of the coming of the Holy Spirit was stated to give the church the power to be witnesses to the ends of the earth. Even the sanctifying enablement of the Holy Spirit was to prepare believers to be more effective and faithful witnesses of Christ and his redeeming power. We are to live out the witness lifestyle both at home and far away. Mission forces of goers and senders, empowered by the Holy Spirit, are certainly needed for the collaborative task of world evangelization. Two parties should strive to create a greater partnership for the church's common task of the Great Commission. After all, both are imperative resources in God's kingdom. One can't excel in the world mission without the other.

> When the Advocate comes, whom I will send to you from the Father—the Spirit of truth who goes out from the Father—he will testify about me. And you also must testify, for you have been with me from the beginning. (John 15:26–27)

In these verses, the Holy Spirit is referred to as the Advocate, which is a legal term. The third person of the Trinity came to testify to the world about the truth that Jesus did not die on a cross for his own sin of treason against the Roman government or blasphemy against Judaism. It is the Spirit who has constantly revealed to the world that Jesus died a substitutionary death for our sins. That is an integral part of the gospel. Jesus invites us to participate in this glorious redemptive venture of the Holy Spirit by saying *"you also must testify."*

GOD'S MISSION

The above texts synthesize to illustrate the Holy Spirit's unending passion to call the lost to salvation. For this cause, he continuously calls out his instruments from the nations and compels them to incubate this world vision. He also empowers them to live it out in every given opportunity. It is God who reminds us that every born-again believer is indebted to the lost world just as Paul confessed himself to be a debtor to everyone (Romans 1:14).

The Spirit of the Lord came upon Isaiah (Isaiah 61:1a) and Jesus (Luke 4:16–21) and likewise comes upon believers today. His coming had an apparent connection with reaching our world, both near and far. Even Isaiah 61 connotes the concept of world mission by ending with the mention of all the "nations." Above all known theories and strategies of world mission, the sovereign work and grace of our God can't be ignored in this endeavor. It is the underlying ingredient of all God-used mission and evangelism efforts in church history. Matthew 24:14 tells us that the "gospel of the kingdom *will* be preached in the whole world as a testimony to all nations, and then the end will come." The word "will" gives us a hint that this enterprise of world mission is eventually a work of the Holy Spirit. Again, Acts 11:21 shows that it was "the Lord's hand" that brought a great number of people to believe and turn to the Lord. Therefore, total dependency on the leading of the Holy Spirit and fellowship with him is an undeniable key for the successful missional enterprise.

COMMUNION OF THE HOLY SPIRIT

In 1995 I was still a young minister back in America. I was at work to establish a ministry base in suburban Washington, DC, for missionary works in Africa. After a year of hard labor in personal discipleship and fundraising, I was getting exhausted at low turnouts and empty promises of people whom I thought I could count on. It seemed I wasn't going anywhere. I was almost coming to a point of giving up on full-time ministry. One frustrating day, I simply collapsed on the carpet and began to sob out of despair. A lament for myself, together with utter complaints toward God, burst out. I wished that God had never called me to ministry and that I had never responded to him in the first place. It wasn't exactly a prayer but more of a lamentation. Hours passed by, if not the whole afternoon. Suddenly, the Holy Spirit gently but firmly impressed my heart with this word. It was the same tugging that had previously led me for years in the past. "Ministry is not your doing. It is my doing. Change your mindset of ministry." I couldn't help but stay right there in the following hours by meditating and processing what he meant by that. I was in a mood of ongoing repentance. By then, it was pretty much my routine to make decisions myself for ministry and afterward go before the Lord in prayer so that he might bless those decisions. I knew I had to change that.

I made a promise to the Lord that day on two things. First, I'd always acknowledge the Holy Spirit as my Senior Leader in ministry. This meant that my team and I would inquire of the Lord before decisions were made in ministry. Prayer meetings began to precede before the board meetings. The culture of asking the Lord for his guidance, both in personal life and ministry directions, was developed. This transformed the course of my ministry. Instead of quarrels, a spirit of unity was soon fostered within my team.

I offered him another prayer of commitment that day: "Lord, if it pleases you, use me to encourage and strengthen your servants elsewhere who are in discouragement and despair, just like I was." The Lord has granted my wish. Every ministry I have been involved in since then has been centered around that scope. God has used me to provide pastoral support, strategic direction, and coaching to the national directors of EAPTC, who oversee ministry operations in fifteen countries. I've been pursuing the same vision through my extensive teaching ministry at several seminaries in Asia.

Not only that, but the ministry base was also established and the support team was erected. I was ready to leave for Africa a year later. If it weren't for that hopelessness I felt in my early ministry, I'd have never fully understood the challenges Christian ministry leaders face and further developed compassion for them. Thousands of disciples raised and hundreds of churches planted as of today trace back to that humble moment of rededication. As it was said, a hardship of yesterday turned out to be the ministry opportunity of today.

Most of all, the Holy Spirit became my Senior Companion in ministry. This was my greatest takeaway. John 14:16, 26; 15:26–27; and 16:7 talk about the powerful communion with the Holy Spirit a believer can have. The Gospel of John is full of great teachings about the role of our beloved Holy Spirit. He is the one who leads our ministry. He is the one who bears fruits in our ministry. He is the one who testifies about Jesus Christ to the world through us. How we work with the Holy Spirit determines either our success or failure in the ministry.

2 Corinthians 13:14 shows us the principle in various versions:

> May the grace of the Lord Jesus Christ, and the love of God, and the fellowship of the Holy Spirit be with you all. (NIV)
>
> The amazing grace of the Master, Jesus Christ, the extravagant love of God, the intimate friendship of the Holy Spirit, be with all of you. (Message)
>
> Ἡ χάρις τοῦ κυρίου Ἰησοῦ χριστοῦ καὶ ἡ ἀγάπη τοῦ θεοῦ καὶ ἡ κοινωνία τοῦ ἁγίου πνεύματος μετὰ πάντων ὑμῶν. (Tyndale House Greek New Testament)

Vocabularies like "fellowship," "intimate friendship," and "κοινωνία" imply that the Holy Spirit can be the greatest and most intimate friend in ministry. We can tell him every problem we face. He will never backbite on us. I've told him countless times about my challenges that turned me down and my adversaries who slandered and persecuted me. He has always comforted me and often changed the hearts of those who got in my way. Cross-cultural gospel workers will need to learn to talk with the Holy Spirit, tell him their problems, and spend time with him. Communion with him will be a lifesaver in ministry.

Prayer is not old-fashioned. Jesus prayed. Early church folks prayed. So should we. There is no alternative idea. In the end, prayer is beneficial to us. We experience freedom from the stress of ministry. I confess I became healthier after learning how to commune with the Holy Spirit. Mary, Queen of Scots, once stated that she feared the prayers of John Knox more than all the assembled armies of Europe. Prayer can move the King of kings and the Lord of lords to act on our behalf as we align our will to his. What an honorable privilege it is and, at the same time, how unfortunate will it be if we disregard to exercise this privilege! We have but every reason to pray, for heaven's sake.

HOLY SPIRIT'S MISSION

We need to commit our daily schedule to God by giving him our first hour of each day. The busier we are, the earlier we need to wake up in the morning to spend more time in prayer. Otherwise, our life will be most likely chased by daily activities that await us. We may not be empowered enough to seize the day. We may lose the sense of Jesus' lordship over the day. Overall, we may end up losing precious time.

Mark 3:14-15 reads, "He [Jesus] appointed twelve—designating them apostles—that *they might be with him* and that he might send them out to preach and to have authority to drive out demons." I'm fascinated by the primary reason Jesus called the Twelve two thousand years ago as well as those of us who are called to serve him today. It was *not* for ministry. He called us *to be with him*. The prerequisite of Jesus' calling is to *have been with him*. It was his primary reason to call the disciples. *Koinonia* (fellowship) with our invisible Lord is correlated with the visible results of our mission and evangelism efforts. This is why it is critical to submit all our missional enterprises to the Lord by prayer, inquiry, and fellowship with his Spirit.

It also shows us how unnecessary we are in a panoramic picture of the *missio Dei*. Nevertheless, the King of kings has graciously decided to share with us his glorious and adventurous kingdom tasks. When we spend time with him, he is the one who will lead us to the very people he wants to reach through us. That will unleash God's power in action to confirm the word with the deed (Mark 16:20). Remembering this key principle will keep us on the right priorities of life. It'll keep us humble to continuously seek the Holy Spirit's fellowship and partnership in everything we do in our world mission outreach. After all, the Holy Spirit *never* fails his mission. The key is, are we willing to acknowledge his leading and learn to cooperate with him?

DISCUSSION AND REFLECTION QUESTIONS

1. John 15:26-27 confirms that Christians are to work with the Holy Spirit in witnessing about Christ to all the world. Examine how you're to do so either as a goer or sender (or maybe both and more) in God's mission.

2. How would you describe your prayer life? See below to describe it accordingly. What can you do strategically to improve your prayer life?

- Dry (no power)
- Warning (unbalanced)
- Enriching (full of power and the Holy Spirit)

3. World mission is eventually the work of the Holy Spirit. Meditate on Mark 3:14–15 and ponder Jesus' primary reason to call his disciples. Lee writes, "It was *not* for ministry. He called us *to be with him*. The prerequisite of Jesus' calling is to *have been with him* . . . *Koinonia* (fellowship) with our invisible Lord is correlated with the visible results of our mission and evangelism efforts." How would you reflect to see this pivotal call answered in your life and ministry?

7

Mobilizing Missionaries from the Nations

WORKERS IN HIS HARVEST FIELD

> The harvest is plentiful but the workers are few. Ask the Lord of the harvest, therefore, to send out workers into his harvest field. (Matthew 9:37–38)

It is God's mission. Jesus is the commander-in-chief of that mission. The Holy Spirit carries out this mission. The triune God has been, is, and will be orchestrating the panorama of world mission. He graciously calls out his servants from the nations to share the harvest he is reaping. God is in the business of calling, equipping, and using anyone from everywhere by sending them everywhere today.

Our God is a missionary God. He is mindful of the global harvest. Even the Son of God chose the perfect time and place of his incarnational birth over two thousand years ago in Bethlehem during the Roman occupation. The Roman Empire succeeded to connect the transportation route between the Middle East, Europe, Asia, and Africa for the first time in history. Christ's message took advantage of the fifty thousand-miles-long Roman roads that led to every corner of the world from the center of Jerusalem. It was culturally unified by the Greek influence so the New Testament could be read by all Greek readers of the time while the Old Testament was mainly accessible to Hebraic Jews. Since the day of Pentecost, the Holy Spirit has been briskly calling and equipping his colaborers from the nations for the world harvest.

SHIFTS IN CHRISTIAN DEMOGRAPHY

The 2004 Lausanne Forum for World Evangelization, held in Pattaya, Thailand, recognized the accelerating growth of churches in the South, namely Africa, Asia, and Latin America. Moreover, church leaders from the South are increasingly demonstrating exemplary leadership for the global body of Christ.[1] As the church of the Global South experienced unprecedented growth and expansion in the past centuries, the number of missionaries and cross-cultural ministry workers from Global South naturally grew.

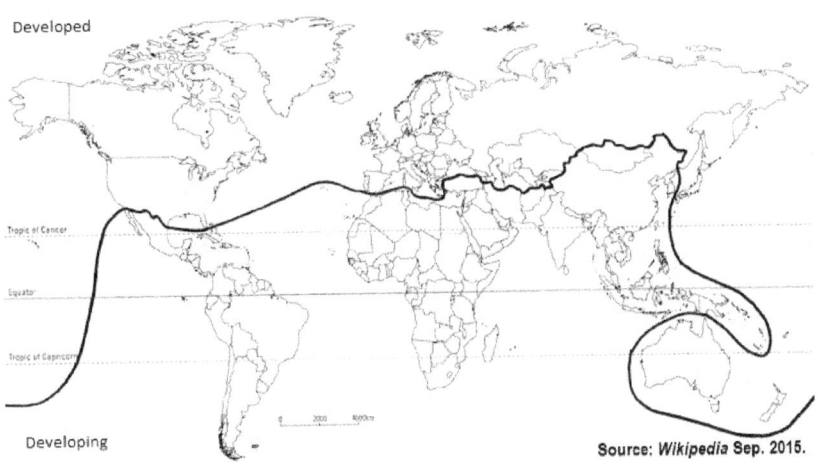

Global North vs. South divide

Christendom undeniably owes a debt to Christian missionaries from the Global North for much of Great Commission endeavors in the twentieth century. Nevertheless, if the man of Macedonia whom Paul encountered in vision were a man of Asia or Africa, the story would have unfolded quite differently. Possibly, it could have been the Global South that enjoyed transformative aspects of blossoming Christian culture for centuries. It is a likely scenario that missionaries from the Global South propagated the gospel to the ends of the earth by the mid twentieth century. However, it

---

1. Claydon, "Context for the Production."

was the Europeans and European settlers at large, anthropologically rightful descendants of Japheth, one of Noah's three sons, who have been used by God for centuries as brave forerunners of world mission throughout history.[2] Unfortunately, the rise of colonialism left a fatal misconception that Christianity paralleled Western propaganda. It was somewhat confusing to differentiate to those oppressed by colonizers of the past because they were both explorers and often shared the same routes to enter their new fields. It took incessant contextualization efforts of devout missionaries and local evangelists who assisted national dissemination of the gospel and the contextualization process to present the message to be faithful to its meaning but be flexible in its function. This effort served as an integral part of the growth of Global South Christendom. The Global South Christian population is on an upward trajectory to become three-fourths of the entire world Christian population by 2100.[3] As the Christian population has increased in the Global South, so naturally has the number of church leaders raised within and missionaries sent out from the region.

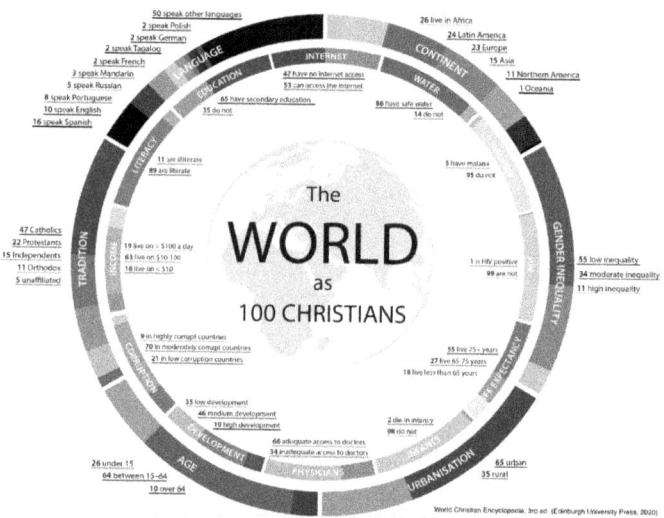

An analysis from the Center for the Study of Global Christianity, a ministry of Gordon Conwell Theological Seminary, shows that things are different now from a hundred years ago. Today, a typical image of a Christian is a non-Caucasian female living in the Global South with low income and poor health care.[4]

2. See Custance, *Noah's Three Sons*.
3. "Gidokgyo hwaksan'gwa segye gidokgyo byeonhwa."
4. Zurlo, "World as 100 Christians."

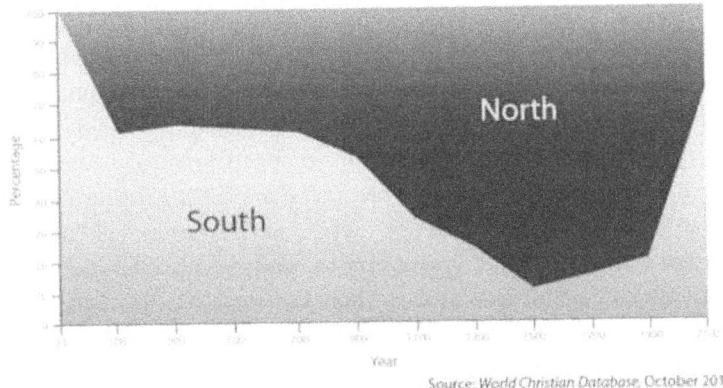

Christians by percentage in North or South, 33-2100 CE

Source: *World Christian Database*, October 2013.

Missionary forces from both Global North and South are certainly needed for the collaborative task of world evangelization.[5] Overcoming differences and prejudices by promoting ethnorelativism rather than ethnocentrism[6] should create a greater partnership for the church's common task of the Great Commission. It is God who called both of them for the world mission, and we need to learn to work together.

Upon ending of the colonial era after World War II, God has been robustly raising Two-Thirds World missionary candidates to come to serve alongside the missionary candidates from the First World. Some of them, however, have carried their unhealed victim mentality into their mission fields and even replicated a neocolonial mindset on the local people they went to serve. Due to the confused, corrupt, and competitive nature of some Two-Thirds World environments, some were likely to carry multiple baggage of sociological, emotional, psychological, and spiritual scars. Missionary candidates must get those scars treated at the predeparture stage. Otherwise, the baggage carried from their previous experiences can seriously affect the overall interpersonal relationship on the field. At IGSL, Eunice and I had the privilege to minister to the training needs of some of the Two-Thirds World missionaries who came for their further study during their furlough. We witnessed that the cultural hybridity of Two-Thirds World missionaries and their kids can also cause them to suffer confusion in defining their identities after years of tenure in the field.

---

5. See Pate, *From Every People*.
6. Moon, "Toward True Globalism in World Missions."

MISSIONARY TRAINING FOR THE NATIONS

While there is a current trend to learn about true globalism in the world missions movement, it is still essential for the body of Christ to consider the crucial need to assist missionary forces with their cross-cultural training need. Along this path, my ministry team and I have developed a missionary predeparture training program with several distinctive features that are sensitive to the Majority World setting where most mission fields still lie today. Afterward, EAPTC opened their missions training schools in Kenya, Tanzania, Malawi, South Korea, China, and Brazil. EAPTC developed a curriculum called Missionary Candidate Training (MCT) and also offered the same course online in cooperation with DCI Global Partnerships in England. The principles of cross-cultural mission presented in the training manual were also partially field-tested in other regions of Africa, Asia, Americas, and Oceania by translating them into French, Spanish, Portuguese, Amharic, and Korean.[7] Later, MCT was validated through quantitative research as effective to enhance a trainee's intercultural readiness.[8] It was through the efforts of those missionary trainees that EAPTC's mission work expanded to numerous church plants in fifteen countries around the world today.[9]

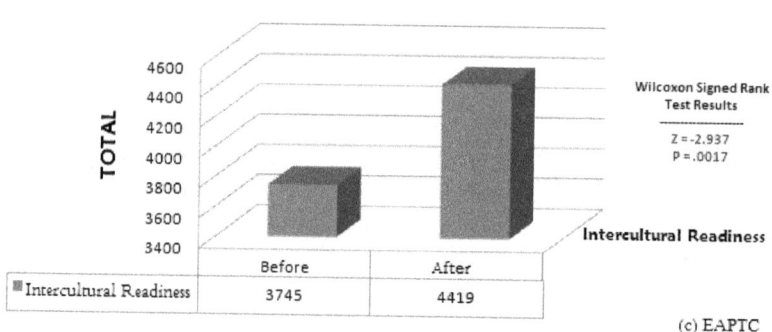

Figure 3. MCT's impact on intercultural readiness

---

7. EAPTC's MCT training manual is available online for purchase at Amazon.com in English, Spanish, French, and Portuguese, and also in Amharic on a personal request to the author by email.

8. For a detail statistical analysis of this research, see Lee, "Impact of Missionary Training on Intercultural Readiness," 52–66.

9. As of August 2019.

One of the most critical components of missionary preparation is intercultural readiness. Leaving for overseas missionary services without enough chances to receive and get tested on cross-cultural preparedness to deal with the locals on the field may result in early attrition, depression, and unfruitful service in the field.[10] According to the exhaustive review of related literature, the four subdomain components that enhance one's intercultural readiness at the predeparture stage were found to be: (1) interpersonal relationships, (2) cultural adaptation, (3) family relationships, and (4) previous experience learning.[11] The enhancement of interpersonal relationships is critical in missionary preparation. Poor interpersonal relationships might cause ineffective, depressive missionary service. Being conversant with cultural adaptation helps missionaries a great deal in that it is less stressful for them and more relational to the locals they work with. Family bonding is critical in any overseas expatriate service. Family support holds its members together during the difficult season of relocation to a new country and adjustment to a new culture. Inward encouragement within the family produces outward synergy for their life in foreign environments. This component likewise affects those who immigrate to other countries for a job, education, marriage, freedom, etc. The sound family relationships of a missionary can be also exemplificative and replicative to local people the missionary works with. Life in the unfamiliar setting of a mission field is expected to involve mistakes and even dilemmas. It is, therefore, wise to learn from those previous experiences that might have been similar to the current challenges.

1. Conceptualization Elements of Missionary Training

Born in Korea and having relocated to America, Africa, and Asia, I experienced firsthand the difficulty of adjusting to new cultures. Intercultural preparation became my life concern and foremost interest to help out anyone wishing to go and serve as a missionary in a cross-cultural context. As I ran missions training courses in multiple world locations for missionary candidates at their predeparture stage, my research expanded and endeavored to get expertized in the area. Ferris identified four characteristics that distinguish the programs of effective missionary training centers. First, effective missionary training centers are consciously and intentionally oriented toward character and skills development for cross-cultural ministry. Stress on the development

---

10. Kim, "Sheer Numbers Do Not Tell the Entire Story," 467–68.

11. For a more exhaustive literature review on the components of intercultural effectiveness, see Lee, "Impact of Missionary Training on Intercultural Readiness," 23–36.

of character and faithfulness underlay the entire MCT program from its orientation process to the last lesson of the training. Second, the effective missionary training center is a living community devoted to developing Christian graces and to refining interpersonal skills. Small-group learning was set to be the mandatory setting for MCT to be implemented regardless of place and time. Third, effective missionary training centers make strategic use of informal and non-formal learning. From academic classes to practica, MCT served its trainees with a down-to-earth yet well-researched teaching program. Fourthly, effective missionary training centers have training curricula appropriate to their task. Hands-on training was implemented to assist its trainees with cross-cultural preparation.[12] In particular, among the many other helpful resources provided, the program was appropriately geared to enhance the trainees' intercultural readiness through various teaching approaches.

The MCT lessons were based on a biblical worldview with an incarnational learning experience, run in a small-group setting of a minimum of five to a maximum of fifteen participants. The community experience developed critical thinking skills, and the praxis components influenced the spiritual growth of participants.[13] Classes portrayed a communal living style, blending non-formal, informal, and formal education of missionaries. After the orientation sessions, the classes normally ran for ten teaching sessions in flexible times and locations. Lessons were conveniently transmitted to suit any world economy setting, with or without high technology involved. MCT worked with local congregations and facilitators to offer classroom experiences, as well as a hands-on internship in the areas where a participant was deemed to need more training after assessments.

2. Small Group Training

The MCT program deliberately ran in small groups to model the principles of discipleship exercised by the first disciples, who spent time with Jesus and heard what Jesus said and continually went under his supervision and did themselves what he did, reporting back to Jesus. They learned by hearing and by doing, and they learned the value of fellowship, working in teams and accountability.[14] This was the model EAPTC adopted to handle the harvest in many countries today, following what Jesus did in Palestine

---

12. Ferris, "Standards of Excellence," 1.
13. Kim, "Dialogical Approach and Spiritual Growth, 159.
14. See Hull, *Disciple-Making Church*.

two thousand years ago. This approach also spared organizers the stress of acquiring a large facility to convene classes and can be used anywhere.

3. Biblical, Non-Western Worldview Training

The MCT lessons were based on biblical, non-Western worldview learning. David Noebel has listed six worldviews that are dominant in the world today: (1) Christian theism, (2) Islamic theism, (3) secular humanism, (4) Marxism, (5) cosmic humanism, and (6) postmodernism.[15] Paul Hiebert stated that worldviews are transformed in two basic ways. "Normal change occurs when changes on the level of conscious beliefs and practices over time infiltrates and brings about change at the *worldview* level."[16] He saw the worldview transformation "as a point, conversion, and as a process, ongoing deep discipling."[17] MCT could easily be adapted into local congregations who wish to experience biblical worldview transformation for those holding existing general worldviews. Here is a diagram showing how one's worldview shifted as he was converted to Christ and matured in Christian discipleship.

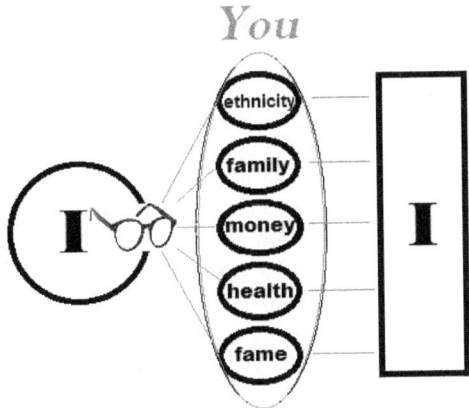

DIAGRAM 1
< General Worldview >

---

15. See Noebel, *Understanding the Times*.
16. Hiebert, *Transforming Worldviews*, 319. Emphasis added.
17. Hiebert, *Transforming Worldviews*, 319.

> So from now on we regard no one from a worldly point of view.
> Though we once regarded Christ in this way, we do so *no longer*.
> (2 Corinthians 5:16)

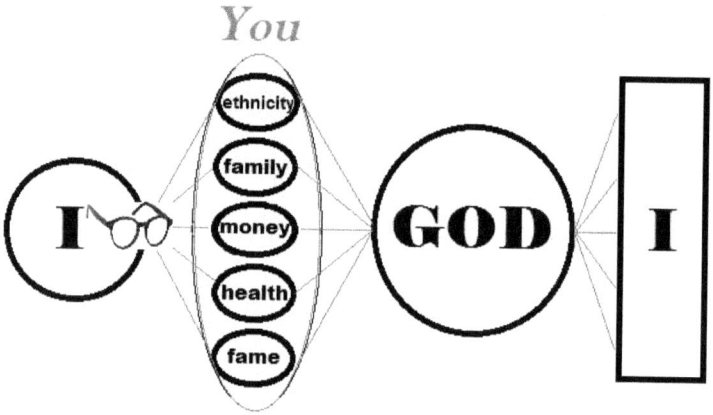

DIAGRAM 2

< Unbiblical Worldview >

While it was generally administered to both Western and non-Western missionary candidates, the missionary candidates directly from the Global South or out of the diasporic background with a Global South heritage were particularly encouraged to experience a transformative shift of worldview during their missionary training. Having seen many missionary trainees coming from a Global South background over the years, EAPTC was keenly in search of practical training curricula with a historically and biblically balanced worldview appropriate for a Majority World perspective, which we believed would be also beneficial for our Western missionary trainees.[18] Training curricula written from a non-Western perspective and a biblically based worldview were in need. Larry D. Pate notes in his article in Ralph Winter's book, *Perspectives on the World Christian Movement*,

> Global cooperation in missionary training is vital. The rapid growth of the Third World missions movement is creating an emergency need for adequate missionary training. While there are some excellent examples of Third World missionary training institutions, many missionaries are sent to the field with little or no training, while others must wait months or even years

---

18. Lewis, "Contextualizing Needs Assessment."

for a training opportunity. But sending a missionary without training is like commissioning a carpenter without tools! With the number of Third World missionaries promising to multiply three and one-half times during this decade, this is a priority issue for Western and non-Western missionary leaders alike.[19]

While, for instance, I believe Global South missionaries have some unique traits to contribute positively toward the Great Commission—the orientation to the supernatural, beliefs concerning the spirit world, gifts of relationship, the concept of the extended family, care for the elderly, concept of hospitality, and event vs. time orientation[20]—their missions trainees lacked a de-Westernized and contextualized training model.

DIAGRAM 3

< Biblical Worldview>

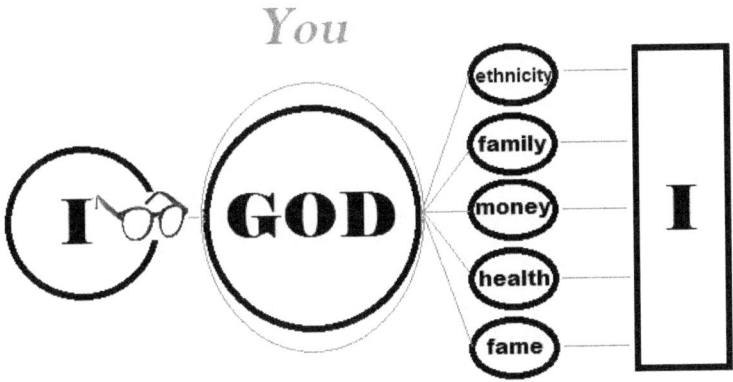

Denis Lane has described four advantages the Majority World missionaries have over their Western counterparts: (1) cultural similarity to the target culture, usually meaning less adjustment is required; (2) access to obtaining a visa to a similar country; (3) more experience in the educational needs, poverty, and difficult political situations of the cultures they are going to; and (4) lack of colonial background.[21] The worldviews of the non-Western world differ from the Western world, which expedited the development of the MCT manual being carefully designed and implemented from the perspective of the Majority World.

19. Pate, "Changing Balance in Global Mission," 60.
20. Lee, *Missionary Candidate Training*, 21–22.
21. Lane, *Tuning God's New Instruments*, 3.

4. Incarnate Homogenization Emphasis Training

MCT also emphasized the need to incarnate homogenization both in theory and practice. An effort toward incarnation was vitally important for the success of the missions.[22] It is necessary to mention the importance of Christ's exemplary incarnational effort, which should be replicated regardless of time and place. The gospel can only be effectively delivered when missionaries understand the people they are trying to reach and the world in which they live. Charles Kraft observed,

> Anthropology has said that in order to study people, we have to observe people by living with them and participating with them in their everyday life. We must live with them, learn their language, and do as much as we can to learn to look at the world from their point of view. We need to discover what their assumptions are concerning reality and ask ourselves questions such as, "If I assumed reality to be what they assume it to be, how would the world look to me? And if it looked that way to me, how would I behave?" On the basis of the understandings gained through seeking answers to such questions, applied anthropologists (including missionaries) have often been able to help people discover answers to problems they previously could not solve.[23]

Many different terms describe elements of "incarnate homogenization" from various disciplines, including developmental psychology, sociology, and ethology. For the clarity of this discussion, existing terminologies from the two most relevant fields, developmental psychology and missiology, are illustrated in Table 1 below.[24]

The concept of incarnation has gained much attention during the last two decades. It was initiated by Kraft[25] and was developed more extensively by Lingenfelter and Mayers.[26] It is based on the incarnation of Christ in Philippians 2:5–8: "Have this mind in you, which was also in Christ Jesus: who, existing in the form of God, counted not the being on an equality with God a thing to be grasped, but emptied himself, taking the form of a servant, being made in the likeness of men; and being found in fashion as a man, he humbled himself, becoming obedient even unto death, yea, the

---

22. Morris, "Coherence of the Incarnation."
23. Kraft, *Anthropology for Christian Witness*, 12.
24. Reisacher, "Processes of Attachment between the Algerians and French."
25. See Kraft, *Christianity in Culture*; Kraft, *Communicating the Gospel*.
26. See Lingenfelter and Mayers, *Ministering Cross-Culturally*.

death of the cross" (ASV). As Jesus became like us to communicate with us, missionaries should apply Jesus' example of the incarnation when they enter and live on the field with a similar ongoing lifestyle and attitude.[27]

Kraft saw the incarnational concept as God's strategy to aid the communication of his message more effectively to the receptors. God employed the most basic principle of effective communication, receptor-oriented communication. This is a principle that all missionaries must learn to imitate in their lives and ministries. Incarnation—personal participation in the lives of his receptors—was the method Jesus constantly modeled. And as in all life-changing communication, the person (whether God himself in Christ or another person as God's representative) was the major component of the message conveyed.[28]

Lingenfelter and Mayers also explained that the incarnation of Jesus Christ could be used as an example and model for missionaries, instructing them to enter into, live in, and minister within the receptors' culture. Likewise, Jesus left his home in heaven to live among and minister to people as a bonded belonger of a particular community, speaking the same language spoken by those living in Palestine at the time. In the same manner, the missionary is born, grows, and lives within the target community by going through the incarnational process.[29]

Christ's incarnation was God's way of meeting humans here on earth. Following his example, missionaries must learn to be at home in a new language and culture they enter—they must become bonded belongers.[30] The purpose of the incarnation was best illustrated by Lingenfelter and Mayers in the following:

---

27. Hiebert, *Anthropological Insights for Missionaries*.
28. Kraft, *Communicating the Gospel*, 17.
29. Lingenfelter and Mayers, *Ministering Cross-Culturally*, 16–17.
30. Brewster and Brewster, "Language Exploration and Acquisition Resource Notebook," 160.

Developmental Psychology			Missiology		
Term	Years	Authors	Term	Years	Authors
Imprinting	1950s	Lorenz[31]	Identification	1950–60s	Nida,[32] Smalley,[33] and Reyburn[34]
Bonding	1970s	Bowlby,[35] Klaus and Kennell[36]	Role Adaptation	1970s	Loewen[37] and Mayers
			Bicultural Community	1980s	Hiebert and Smith[38]
Attachment/ Attachment bonding	1980–90s	Bowlby,[39] Ainsworth,[40] Sroufe,[41] and Schore[42]	Bonding	1980s	Brewsters
			Incarnation	1980s	Charles Kraft and Lingenfelter
Immersion	1980s	Marshall[43]	Attachment	2000s	Reisacher

Table 1. Comparison between two approaches:
Developmental psychology and missiology

The reason that incarnation (i.e., a willingness to begin to learn as if we are helpless infants) is necessary for intercultural ministry lies in the nature of cultural learning and perception. Culture is always learned and shared with others, and in this process people begin to perceive and respond to one another in culturally conditioned ways.[44]

31. Lorenz, "Kumpan in der Umwelt des Vogels."
32. See Nida, *Message and Mission*.
33. Smalley, "Cultural Implications of an Indigenous Church."
34. Reyburn, "Identification in the Missionary Task."
35. See Bowlby, *Making and Breaking of Affectional Bonds*.
36. See Klaus and Kennell, *Maternal-Infant Bonding*.
37. Loewen, Culture and Human Values, 400.
38. "Missiological Abstracts."
39. See Bowlby, *Attachment*.
40. Ainsworth and Bowlby, "Ethological Approach to Personality Development," 333.
41. Sroufe, "Coherence of Individual Development," 834.
42. Schore, "Attachment and the Regulation of the Right Brain."
43. See Marshall and Wieling, "Promoting MFT Diversity."
44. Lingenfelter and Mayers, *Ministering Cross-Culturally*, 22.

Missionary incarnation through bonding with local people opens the ultimate pathway to cross-cultural discipleship.⁴⁵ Incarnational ministry in this global age catalyzes respect, humility, and leadership by learning from brothers and sisters of different backgrounds and heritages.⁴⁶

The Lord often causes and orchestrates the movement of people and cultural groups to other geographic locations of the world, although their initial reasons may vary. Again, Acts 17:26 palpably confirms that it was *the Lord* who determined their preappointed times and the boundaries of their dwellings. This was the third conceptualization element stressed in the MCT manual.

5. Missionary Longevity

Preparing missionary candidates with sufficient intercultural resilience is believed to be essential for longevity on the mission field.⁴⁷ While unpreventable departures of missionaries from the field might be unstoppable—e.g., retirement, death, loss of visa, and appointment to leadership in the mission agency—there were preventable causes that forced missionaries to leave the field—e.g., work- or team-related reasons, dismissal, personal issues, and agency issues.⁴⁸ Concerning the top four factors that contributed the most to missionaries effectively attaining their tasks on the field, seventy-five of the seventy-eight mission agencies in the United States responded: (1) development of good relationships/team (thirty-two agencies), (2) commitment to the ministry (twenty-seven agencies), (3) effective leadership with good supervision and accountability (twenty-five agencies), and (4) clear objectives, goals, and expectations that were agreed upon (twenty-four agencies). When the same agencies were asked about the factors that hindered missionaries the most from attaining effectively their tasks on the field, seventy-four of the seventy-eight agencies noted the top factors as: (1) a lack of finances (thirty agencies), (2) family issues (twenty-eight agencies), and (3) relationship problems (twenty-seven agencies).⁴⁹

The preventable causes of forced departure from mission fields, including interpersonal relationship conflicts and family discords, might be remedied if there were adequate training focusing on intercultural preparation provided before missionaries leave for the field.

45. Malina, *Christian Origins and Cultural Anthropology*, 70.
46. Moon, "Toward True Globalism in World Missions."
47. Brynjolfson, "Effective Equipping of the Cross-Cultural Worker," 75–77.
48. World Evangelical Alliance, "ReMAP II," 10.
49. Van Meter. "US Report of Findings on Missionary Retention."

EFFECTIVE MISSIONARY TRAINING

According to this research, missionary training that was carefully designed to provide an emphasis on small-group learning, biblical and non-Western worldviews, and incarnate homogenization should prepare missions trainees practically and result in a significant increase in their intercultural readiness in the subdomain components of interpersonal relationships, cultural adaptation, family relationships, and previous experience learning.

Interpersonal relationships, cultural adaptation, family relationships, and previous experience learning play the integral roles in missionary's cross-cultural preparation. All in all, MCT was designed and developed to suit the above exclusive specifics to improve the intercultural readiness in one's missionary predeparture preparation. The purpose of eminence in the intercultural preparation was for sound and effective tenure in the mission field with greater longevity and fruitful task performance in one's missionary service; thus, there might be less crash and burn because of cultural differences.

Both the Global South and North have a role to play in world mission. While the Lord is on the move to call out more missionary forces from the church of the Global South, the church of Global North may seriously and tactically consider helping missionary candidates of their Global South counterpart partners in the areas of adequate missionary training, including financial contributions toward it. The church of the Global North may need to overcome paternalistic approaches as they come alongside to partner with missionary candidates of the Global South. Borthwick suggests five paternalisms to recede in this regard: (1) resource paternalism, (2) spiritual paternalism, (3) knowledge paternalism, (4) labor paternalism, and (5) managerial paternalism.[50]

Missionary trainers at local churches and other cross-cultural mission agencies are encouraged to provide a predeparture mission training that emphasizes small-group learning, biblical worldview, and incarnate homogenization, and in turn contribute toward the assessment and development of missionary training programs that are sensitive to the need of tactile intercultural preparation to minister in the Majority World setting. In the end, a collaborative teamwork of sharpened missionary forces from both the Global North and South will thrive further and penetrate deeper in this unprecedented day and age when people move from everywhere to everywhere and the gospel propagates from everywhere to everywhere.

---

50. Borthwick, *Western Christians in Global Mission*, 152–53.

This chapter shows how a missionary training program appropriate to the Majority World setting was developed. Emphasis on small-group learning, biblical and non-Western worldviews, and incarnational mission produces a significant increase in the intercultural readiness of trainees. It has made the missionaries produced by EAPTC more effective in their intercultural encounters and also reduced the stress they underwent in crossing cultures. They were cross-culturally prepared and attested in the domains of interpersonal relationships, cultural adaptation, family relationships, and learning capacity by experiences.

In parallel with the training ministry of missionary candidates from the nations, EAPTC offered the Senders Course training to local churches upon request. My international team endeavored to raise awareness of missions involvement and to foster strategic missions giving in local churches. Setting up a separate savings account for the missions account was advised to local churches. Tangible financial planning through the monthly reserve was encouraged to aspiring short-term missionaries. Responsive local pastors prayerfully set apart Mission Sundays to teach their congregations about the importance of missions involvement. Short-term mission teams were regularly sent out for ministry tours from partnering local churches. Pastors were first encouraged to go visit mission fields. Elders and deacons would follow in their footsteps. Youths were ultimately challenged to go as well. Upon their return from the short-term mission trip, they were encouraged to give testimony of blessings to get involved in the missions. Missionary vision had to be mutually imparted in the congregational vision of local church leaders; otherwise, biblical missions would not be complete. Missionaries might face limitations in their fieldwork and find it difficult to unfold their cross-cultural call full-fledged without the financial support of local churches and individuals. Having this practical issue in mind, missionary candidates with bivocational skills were given priority for the field commission, especially with the Two-Thirds World missionaries, who might not enjoy strong financial backup from their local churches in developing countries.

In the task of world mission, both goers and senders are mutually important. Without one the other cannot exist, and both need adequate training to effectively discharge Christ's irrevocable command to go and make disciples of all nations. Someone has to preach the message to the nations, and that someone has to be sent, as firmly instructed in Romans 10:14–15.

FROM EVERYWHERE TO EVERYWHERE THROUGH EVERYWHERE

It should be noted that Christian discipleship is, and has been, circulating the globe in history. A great number of dedicated missionaries from the Global North are still reaching out to the rising needs of this hurting world. At the same time, it is no longer uncommon today to witness missionaries from the Global South re-evangelizing secularized Europe and the Global North. The body of Christ needs to respond sensitively and carefully to this global trend. No longer do we have proprietary missionary-sender countries as in the past. The global body of Christ is at the invitation of the Commander-in-Chief of world missions and is responding to it.

As the Holy Spirit continues to shine the light of the gospel through his servants called from everywhere to everywhere, it continually formulates a combination of pure gospel and culturally contextualized elements upon entry to a new field. Incorrect cross-cultural adjustment leads to a cultural gospel instead of the contextualized gospel to the culture. Contextualization can only take place when the gospel message is understood and applies biblical revelation to local culture. People and cultures have been coexisting from the beginning. Genesis, the very first book of the Bible, states that cultures were made by people and conversely. Ironically, the same people later get influenced by the culture they have created.[51]

A cultural gospel isn't the same as the contextualized gospel. Such a phenomenon is repeatedly displayed on every continent. To give an illustration, the American gospel should be differentiated from the gospel that is contextualized into American culture. If the gospel content you preach to affluent upper-class New Yorkers cannot be preached for any reason to devastated refugees sheltering at Kakuma camp in Kenya, you're probably preaching a cultural gospel, not the pure gospel that is contextualized into a culture. The gospel contextualized for New Yorkers can be also contextualized for African refugees. That is the beauty of the pure gospel. Of course, decoding incrementally added elements of a cultural gospel must take place before recoding it with another contextualization effort to make the gospel relevant to a new culture. We'll talk more about the suggested methodology of contextualization in chapter 9.

This notion of serving a global God calls for a global team player. Both at EAPTC and IGSL, Eunice and I have the privilege to serve with the teams that are composed of leaders from various nations. Their expressions of emotion, time concept, and national customs are variant

---

51. Kraft, "Culture, Worldview and Contextualization," 385.

indeed. It is almost impossible to work with an international team of leaders and achieve common success without understanding the emotions of the team members. To work harmoniously with an international team, this thought must not leave one's mind: *Why does he do it the way he does?* Constant consideration of bicultural or tricultural understanding is a virtue of international teamwork. Filipino coworkers are known to have multiple ways to say no without actually saying the word. Most American coworkers will freely express their ideas and feelings with zero intention to offend anyone. However, for many Asians there is a fine line between the presentation of differing opinions and personal offense in debates. Nonverbal communication sometimes voices out louder than verbal communication in international meetings. Intercultural misunderstanding and conflict occasionally do occur. Nonetheless, in Christ's school of kingdom lifestyle, global Christians need to learn how to live and work together.

Every culture has merit to contribute to the growth of the body of Christ. Focusing on others' cultural merits can keep an international team moving toward the common vision and mission. The gift of speech and an optimistic attitude are but two of the many merits of African coworkers I work with. The gentleness of smiling Filipino coworkers brightens my days time and again. The thoughtfulness and discretion of my coworkers from the Far East add prudence in the decision-making process. The practicality of American coworkers and bravery of European coworkers stand out to upgrade the ministry to the next level. The witty straightforwardness of my coworkers from Oceania illuminates brighter in some of the meetings with slow progress. This is only a shadowy depiction of the completed body of Christ in heaven. Everyone using their God-given talents to serve one another with no selfish ambition and giving all the glory to the Lamb who redeemed us and the nations with his sacrificial death on the cross must be what Christ had in mind when he once taught us to pray: ". . . as it is in heaven" (Matthew 6:10).

There must be international cooperation and involvement for the cause of the Great Commission. No one denomination, no one church, no one parachurch organization, and no one highly gifted individual can do it alone. We also need missionaries from both the Global North and the Global South. Global South missionaries have several advantages to connect with the Majority World more intimately. Simultaneously, Global North Christianity can share with Global South missionaries from their rich experiences and practical advice in world missions. Luke 11:42 gives us wise counsel: ". . . you should have practiced the latter without leaving the former undone."

DISCUSSION AND REFLECTION QUESTIONS

1. In the current perspective of global shifts in the missions workforce, what could you do to contribute toward the world mission as a Christian living in the Global North or the Global South?

2. What do you think is the difference between the pure gospel that is contextualized into a culture and a cultural gospel? Examine this in your own cultural context.

3. How would you behave differently as a follower of Christ if you were to work with a multicultural team for ministry or business?

PART III

Called for the Nations

8

Worldview Matters

WHY WORLDVIEW?

Person A and person B, who live in the same world, can still feel as if they're from different worlds because they have different worldviews, not a different world. One's worldview certainly controls his behaviors in the world he sees. Worldview screens everything in a person's life, from A to Z and from life to death.

A cross-cultural ministry worker needs to work first and foremost on viewing people as just people who bear God's image before he views their racial background. As a matter of fact, the Bible, the eternal Word of God, speaks of only two human races God himself has created: male and female (Genesis 1:27; 5:2). Studies show that males and females apparently ascribe to different cultural distinctives in multiple ways.[1] In the Scriptures, there is no categorization of races apart from this. All humans are descended from Adam. It is a matter of skin pigmentation (melanin) and geographical climate that makes us look somewhat different. Today's vocabularies like whites, blacks, yellows, and reds aren't exactly compatible with the biblical concept of race. The modern term "race" actually points to people of different cultures based on the fact that they have lived for generations in lands far away and thus developed different appearances, customs, and views of life.

Global leadership begins with a global mind. A global mind is incubated by a global worldview. A benefit of serving Christ in global

---

1. Wood and Eagly, "Cross-Cultural Analysis," 699.

contexts includes the inevitable enlargement of one's worldview. Indeed, the world is in Christ's hand as the old song declared it so well: "He's got the whole world in his hand!" Yes, he has. The entire world is God's world just as all truths are God's truths. This critical concept leads us to worldview matters for the sake of incubating *all nations*, for whom Jesus died.

Worldview is simply a way we look at the world. It is like glasses. If one's glasses are tinted, the world may look like the color of the glasses' tint. If they're tainted, everything in the world may seem tainted to him. The only untainted glasses to view the world through are the lens of the unbiased Scriptures. The Scriptures display a layout of the way human beings ought to live. Hence, a biblical worldview and healthy contextualization form the two most fundamental capstones to establish a successful cross-cultural discipleship ministry.

Even the way people came up with world maps has gone through a dramatic development if you compare the following maps from AD 150, AD 1154, and AD 1832. We can see that the way people look at the world has also grown and matured, from abstract to accurate.[2]

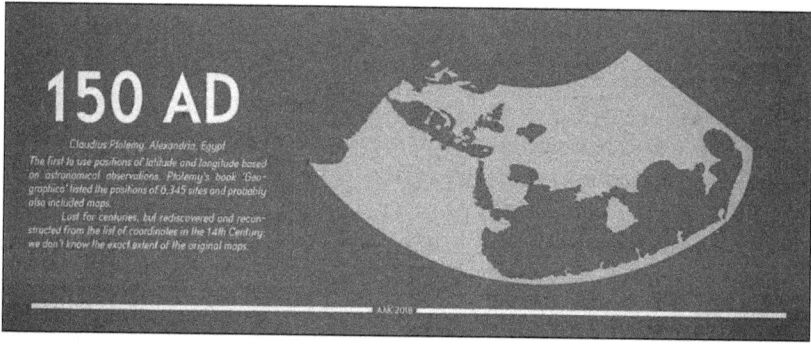

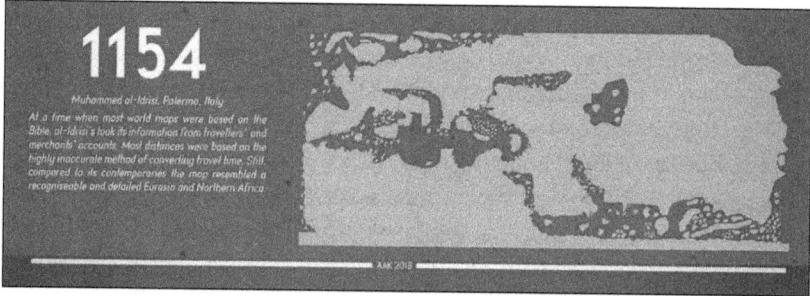

---

2. Ghosh, "Shape of the World."

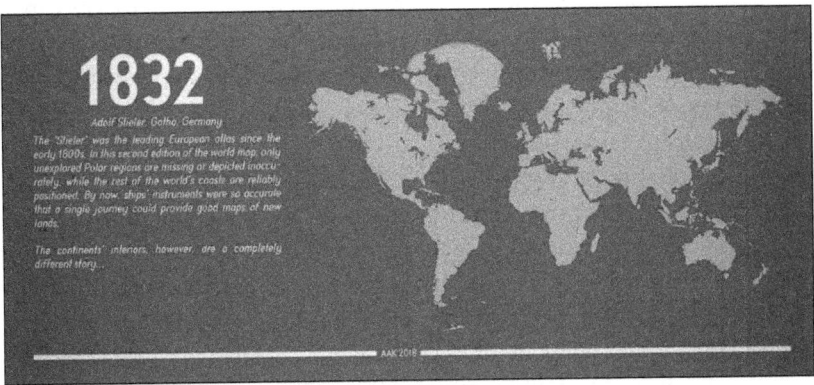

We must possess God's view of our surroundings, our community, and our world. Should we wish to embrace the world for Christ in our hearts, I suggest that we start each day by prayerfully navigating through the world news in the morning. They're unprecedentedly and conveniently available on our smartphones now at the convenience of our fingertips. Followed by morning devotion, my daily routine usually begins by scanning through the headlines of major online newspapers of the Philippines, China, Vietnam, Kenya, the United States, and South Korea. These are some of the countries where my international teams currently operate. This practice helps me feel what my coworkers face and go through each day. Only then can my ministry to provide mentorship to national leaders remain tactile and be counted contemporary and effective as well.

Anyone aspiring to live missionally is encouraged to develop a habit of reflecting on Christ's view on daily matters. It is a process of critical contemplation. God reminds us eighty-two times in the Bible (KiJV) to "consider." The thoughts, speech, and behaviors of a person are determined by his worldview regardless of gender and age. Worldview is a powerful mechanism that shapes one's life value. Three "M"s set the order of his life. One's *meaning* begets his *mission*. One's *mission* begets his *methods*. Matthew 13:44 narrates about this in detail:

> The kingdom of heaven is like *treasure* hidden in a field. When a man found it, he hid it again, and then in his joy went and sold all he had and bought that field.

People invest everything in what they value the most. Whatever they *treasure* is vested with the meaning of their life. This meaning provides them a sense of purpose and mission. Based on their mission, people come up with various methods to pursue their life meaning. This process forms one's worldview. The man who appears in Matthew 13:44 was definitely a man on a mission, and his mission was to purchase a field that hid treasure in it. The hidden treasure has just bestowed a meaning to him. He esteemed the newly found treasure worthy of all his investment of time and resources. This clever man quickly adjusted and carefully planned out his methods to accomplish the mission. First, he'd hide the very treasure back on the field and would aptly disguise as if he was just buying land. He might have negotiated the land's price with the owner before he left. On the way home, he might have reflected on his financial plan to come up with the budget for the price of the field. As soon as he reached home, there is a high possibility that he went ahead and reconfirmed the value and ownership of the field to make sure he was after something genuine. Likely hurried to explain to his family why he had to swiftly sell everything at home, his mind must have been occupied to locate buyers of his quick sale items. He'd not want to waste one more day lest someone else might take the field before him. Imagine the emotional rollercoaster of every anxiety, excitement, and expectation he must have gone through until he finally reached the field owner again to sign the deal and payed for the field in full! Jesus depicts through this practical parable that people can think and act quite differently based on what they value. This is the power of worldview.

IMPACT OF THE WORLDVIEW ON MISSIONS

A fair percentage of leaders whom God used greatly in redemptive history were men and women with global minds. Stephen's systematic sermon before his martyrdom in Acts 10 highlights that the work of God is not confined by any facility, place, country, culture, ethnicity, and even our ministry territory. Thus, being cross-cultural is an intentional nature of God's work. It seems undeniable to say that many God-used individuals in the *missio Dei* were culturally hybrid because of their exposure to multicultural experiences by immigration, exile, asylum, marriage, adoption, education, slavery, colonization, etc. A great number of the culturally hybrid, who carry mixed and multiple identities due to their cross-cultural, intercultural, and multicultural backgrounds, often find themselves challenged to define their "home" but end up discovering their true home and identity in the Lord. Plenty of examples are found in the Bible such as Abraham (Jew in Ur, Haran, Canaan and Egypt), Joseph (Egyptian Jew), Moses (Egyptian Jew), Daniel (Babylonian Jew), and the Seven (Hellenistic Jews) in the early church. Even the apostle Paul had two cultural identities by birth—a Jew born as a Roman citizen. Saul was his Hebrew name while Paul was his

Latin name. He didn't exactly change his name from Saul to Paul as some people think: ". . . Saul, who was *also* called Paul . . ." (Acts 13:9)

Yet, when he was more exhaustively used by the Lord in ministry for Gentiles, he was likely made known more with his Roman identity. All of them were exposed to and familiar with multiple cultures and ethnicities. A broader worldview was incubated in their hearts to bless the nations. Cultural exposure can be an agent of positive and godly influence for Christ.

Sheep beget sheep, and people beget people. People usually share the gospel with other people who are alike and who have a common denominator with them. People with a multicultural worldview can lead people of different cultural backgrounds to Christ. Paul, presumably fluent in multiple languages such as Greek, Hebrew, and possibly Latin, wrote one-third of the New Testament and left a legacy of striking influence among both the Jewish and Gentile world. On the other hand, Peter was likely fluent in Hebrew and only knew basic Latin or Greek. Even some of his two New Testament epistles could have been written with the help of Silas, a Hellenistic Jew (1 Peter 5:12). It is also noteworthy that Peter hesitated twice to align himself with the vision for the Gentile ministry (Acts 10:10–16). On the contrary, Paul responded immediately to the vision of the Macedonian call (Acts 16:9–10). Paul was a cross-cultural agent of the gospel in his DNA. He must have understood that both pros and cons of cultures could be used as a channel for indigenous discipleship. Acts 17:16–34 records his cross-cultural analogy in his missionary journey to Athens. Paul was well aware of the Greek mythology and became conversant to use an altar dedicated to "an unknown god" to connect with the gospel message. It eventually won the hearts of some people to Christ as Acts 17:34 verifies:

> Some of the people became followers of Paul and *believed*. Among them was Dionysius, a member of the Areopagus, also a woman named Damaris, and a number of others.

WORLDVIEW AND THE BIBLE

When asked to name an order of map direction, most North Americans and Europeans refer to them as north, south, east, and west. Koreans and Asians at large are likely to refer to them as east, west, south, and north. Why? For North Americans and Europeans, their world starts from the north. For many Asians, it starts from the east.

In the West, a traditional list of immediate basic human needs is ordered differently from the East. It is usually listed as food, clothing, and shelter. Practical need settles their priorities in the West. The East usually indicates clothing first, and food and shelter follow the list. In many parts of the East, falling under a face-saving cultural zone, outer appearance and social image are often deemed more a priority than the practical need of food. It may not be easy for some Westerners to understand that. However, if you and I consider *why* they do what they do, it begins to open a glimpse of effective cross-cultural communication. The *why* is their worldview.

From a great political leader to a tiny babe on this planet, worldview steers behavior and decision-making. The only problem is that none of us has a holistic worldview on our own. Limited by personal bias, prejudice, and preferences, we all have blind spots. Most of all, humans can't see one's heart. Jeremiah 17:9–10 describes one's heart as the most deceptive thing, and the Lord examines men's hearts and minds. The solely reliable worldview is that of the Bible and its prescribed principles. Postmodernism and subsequentially related worldviews that have sprung up in modern days challenge this idea. Yet, the Bible and its principles have preeminently stood the test of time and kept changing lives for better, transcending time and space.

This practice may go even further by considering one's own ethnicity as the standard for others as well. We should not undermine the fact that one's worldview gravitates to different centers—their own centers. Whether we like it or not, the world doesn't center around you and me. It evolves around the sovereign providence and redemptive plan of our God, who is fervently at work on the fulfillment of the *missio Dei*. Ethnocentrism acutely tampers the basis of biblical mission. The body of Christ was given the missional mandate to reach out "to the ends of the earth." This task calls for a resilient servant-stewardship to go serve even people of uncomfortable cultural behaviors and vexing customs. Only by God's grace and by imitating the humility of Christ can we grow into the maturity of embracing the world with the Lord's unpolluted lens. It will be virtually impossible for anyone with ethnocentrism.

Ezekiel 5:5 mentions that our Lord has set Jerusalem in the center of the nations with countries all around her. While most of us tend to highlight our own nation and ethnicity as the center of the world, the eternal God seems to have a slightly different idea in this regard. It is undeniably a historical truth that the panorama of the Middle East has been leveraging world peace. Israel has been always the powder keg of the world. Being a brake device of the world's peace, the premiers and politicians of the nations have kept their eyes on the Middle East throughout history. No matter how false it may look, the truth is still the truth. No matter how attractive it may look, falsehood is falsehood.

RENEWING THE WORLDVIEW

Christ's command for us to follow him by carrying our cross does not imply that we're under coercion to do so. He desires our cheerful response to this commitment by renewing our worldview. Romans 12:2 reminds us to be transformed by the renewing of our minds. It continues to say that doing so will lead us to discern God's "good, pleasing, and perfect will." Such experiences ought to result in bona fide discipleship instead of artificial religiosity.

The Lord of the universe, Jesus Christ, proclaims that knowing the truth will set us free in John 8:32. Our life is wrapped by thick layers of non-truths to the point that one might even find it hard to tell between truths and non-truths in this crooked generation. From the perspective of the biblical record, the concept of clothing originated from men's hiding of their true state (Genesis 3:7). It wasn't due to the cold or heat of the weather. This leads us to the point that people should not be judged by the way they're dressed. External fine dress does not necessarily correlate to internal decency of the heart. A ton of such cases is found around us these days. Boastful desire gets frequently fueled by the unwillingness to acknowledge truth. Excessive makeup and cosmetic surgery find their root in averting one's eyes from one's true self. A desire to look nice and beautiful is perfectly okay, but an urge to disguise one's true appearance is likely a byproduct of distorted self-image.

The present-day porn phenomenon is but another example. It is a definite degradation of God's gift of sex to men and women. First Timothy 6:17 affirms us to put our hope in God, who richly provides us with *everything* for our enjoyment. Porn severely hampers its viewers from experiencing the maximum sexual pleasure intended by God for a married couple. The genuine ecstasy of sex is utterly deteriorated in porn. Once the biblical view of sex is ruined, social vice gets to be created by the effects of porn. A healthy and satisfying sex life becomes no longer possible in real marriage after the contents of porn occupy one's mind. Real sex life just doesn't match the acts performed in porn. It is simply a distortion of the biblical view of sex. Similarly, most of the bed scenes in today's movies vividly portray sex outside of marriage as a cultural norm. Actors usually act in movies as if their sexual behavior is gratifying each other. This is another non-truth that has deceived and misled millions of young people. Nothing can be further from the truth.

A study in the United States shows that married couples have sex more frequently than singles or cohabitants. The more astounding finding is that sex is better among religious/spiritual married couples than any other category of sexually active people. An interesting correlation was discovered between a couple's religious commitment level and their sex frequency/satisfaction. 32 percent of conservative evangelical women were reported to experience orgasm during sex. Mainline Protestants and Catholics followed them closely with a 27 percent mark. Only 22 percent of the non-religious group was reported to reach orgasm during sex.[3] This study clearly indicates that popular bed scenes in movies that promote sex outside of marriage and self-gratifying porn images foster nothing but falsehood about real sex. They're but a deterioration of the best sex life God has intended for men and women.

God created sex and is willing to lavish its blessing to mankind. That is why the same God also gave us a guideline. The Bible talks about it in plenty of places. The Song of Songs speaks out even louder than other books in this regard. We should not forget that God's guideline enables far more satisfying sex and produces fulfilling sexual pleasure because he is the author of it. Deuteronomy 24:5 talks about how God values marital intimacy in marriage: "When a man takes a new wife, he shall not go out with the army nor be charged with any duty; he shall be free at home one year and shall give happiness to his wife whom he has taken" (NASB). Why does the author of sex guide us to wait for marriage to enjoy lovemaking? Sex outside of marriage lacks commitment, which is a vital element that keeps fueling ongoing love for a couple to pursue realistic happiness and produce mutual sexual pleasure. All other views on sex eventually fall short of the perfect definition of *lovemaking*.

The Bible proclaims that human beings are the image of God. Both male and female bear God's imprint in their soul. Any other views on people will certainly lead us to the falsehood of human identity. As long as human life is viewed as a byproduct of stardust that came about some billions of years ago by a cosmological accident, we're far from treating other people and races as they deserve to be treated. If people are merely the most advanced species among all the animals on earth, there is no rationale to faithfully love our spouse till death do us apart since most animals are polygamous. Worldview dramatically changes one's way of life. While evolutionary theory has been repeatedly challenged by scientific discoveries,[4] many people just haven't been willing to acknowledge the blind spot and to give a fair probe on both evolutionism and creationism, even in academia.

Worldview truly matters. The practice of considering all things with a biblical worldview will put us on the right track. Viewing everything as

---

3. Larimore, "Poll Shows Sex within Marriage Is More Fulfilling."
4. See Rohde, "On the Common Ancestors of All Living Humans."

intended by God should guide us to pursue truths instead of non-truths. It also demands our constant intentionality to see things around us with God's perspective. That is a renewed worldview.

WORLDVIEW, LIFE-VIEW, AND ETERNITY-VIEW

> Now, brothers and sisters, I want to remind you of the gospel I preached to you, which you received and *on which you have taken your stand*. (1 Corinthians 15:1)

This scripture lays a foundation of why Christians do what they do. The gospel and its perspectives must become our stand. You and I are called to live missionally because of this biblical stand. We're supposed to live in the gospel. In turn, we're to live out the gospel. Our worldview, life-view, and eternity-view should be realigned by the gospel perspectives. That is a mission-driven life.

There is a well-known folktale in the Far East. Born and grown inside of a deep well, a frog always enjoyed the comfort and contentment he found at the bottom of the well. A mossy wall of three feet in diameter and the blue sky he occasionally looked upon were literally the world to him. Sometimes, the birds came and told him about the mountains, forest, rivers, and sea, but he wouldn't understand nor believe such things existed. One day, a frustrated sparrow took the frog on his back and flew out of the well. It was a life-changing experience for the frog to witness how big the world was. His view of the world was finally challenged and dramatically enlarged for the first time in his life.

When Christ enters a person's life and takes the steering wheel of his heart, Christ's worldview is concurrently incubated in the person and the person gets on the course toward Christian maturity (Ephesians 4:13). The question is, how large is the scale of Christ's worldview?

> Who has measured the waters in the hollow of his hand, or with the breadth of his hand marked off the *heavens*? . . . (Isaiah 40:12f)

Isaiah recounts the immeasurable scale of our Lord's power and glory, which holds the universe together in his hand. Just the thought of it is enough to blow our minds away beyond the compass of our wildest imagination. When we genuinely take a stand on the gospel and its life-changing power, we can't help but experience the transformation of our worldview. It may be compared to what the frog in the well must have experienced the moment he left his good old well. The world is not worthy of such people who underwent a transformation of this magnitude. Hebrews 11:38 describes them: "The world was not worthy of them . . ."

Christ's worldview challenges and stretches us even further. Daniel 12:3 reminds us of this conviction:

> Those who are wise will shine like the brightness of the heavens, and *those who lead many to righteousness*, like the stars for ever and ever.

It highlights the significance of people because they hold eternal worth. People are valued like nothing else in the biblical worldview. They are, after all, the image of God. Jesus came and died for *people*. A disciple-maker must learn to value people before anything else, even including ministry. There is no ministry without building people first. So is the biblical mission. It is about people. The mission is a people-growing business, both at home and on the field. Confucius once said, "If you want one year of prosperity, grow grain. If you want ten years of prosperity, grow trees. If you want one hundred years of prosperity, grow people."[5] If you and I want an eternity of prosperity, we need to grow people for the cause of Christ. In this perspective, a mission station is not primarily about a building but the dynamic local people who stand with a missionary in vision. Do you value people and grow people because of their eternal value?

WORLDVIEW AND CULTURAL ZONES

Having visited and ministered in over forty nations by this time, my experience confirms that worldview significantly contributes to geographical spiritual strongholds and vice versa. Thus, ethnographic research is highly useful upon a missionary's entry to the field. Regions of Africa that suffer from continual tribal clashes have ethnocentric worldviews heavily rooted in tribes at feud. The areas still in the practice of the horrid act of female genital mutilation (FGM) are often associated with the worldview of degradation of women and their rights. Cities with a high suicidal rate have a close link to people's dominant life-view that believes in reincarnation. To figure out proper means of cross-cultural adjustment in any culture, a gospel worker preliminarily needs to figure out the nature of the spiritual principality affecting the particular region. Therefore, fervent prayers, both personal and corporate, need to serve as a concrete foundation of every cross-cultural ministry endeavor. About geographical spiritual strongholds, Ephesians 6:12 depicts it this way:

5. Landskroner, *Nonprofit Manager's Resource Directory*, 2.

> For our struggle is not against flesh and blood, but against (1) the *rulers*, against (2) the *authorities*, against (3) the *powers* of this dark world and against (4) the *spiritual forces of evil* in the heavenly realms.

Besides, I formerly discussed the research on three major world cultural zones: the honor-shame cultural zone, power-fear cultural zone, and innocence-guilt cultural zone. Those cultural zones are byproducts of regional worldviews, too. To illustrate it, take a look at the jails in different cultural zones. Notably, the design of jails isn't the same. In world areas with an honor-shame culture or innocence-guilt culture, most jails are barred so prisoners may be seen from outside to provoke shame and guilt in them. However, many jails have a different design for those incarcerated in a power-fear culture. They're completely sealed and unseeable from outside. This is to promote fear of prisoners rather than shame or guilt feelings. The impact of the worldview on society is more reflective than we imagine.

SELF-VIEW

Lyman Reed[6] defined an effective missionary as one who has training and natural abilities enabling him to adjust to a new culture, including self-acceptance. Only the person with sound self-acceptance and healthy self-care knows how to love others even across cultures. Matthew 22:36–40 decisively reminds us of this.

> Teacher, which is the greatest commandment in the Law? Jesus replied, "Love the Lord your God with all your heart and with all your soul and with all your mind." This is the first and greatest commandment. And the second is like it: "Love your neighbor *as yourself*." All the Law and the Prophets hang on these two commandments.

It should be noted that the Bible does not command us to love our neighbor with all our heart, soul, and mind. It simply tells us to love them as we love ourselves. Loving oneself is, therefore, foundational for loving neighbors and even loving God. However, a lot of people do not know how to truly love themselves. It might as well be the happy feelings they sense that they love, not necessarily themselves. If you and I truly love ourselves, we should be able to exercise "tough love" sometimes even for ourselves. If one craves sweets but is diabetic, allowing himself the sweets for temporal happiness is not true love. Watching porn to indulge the lust of one's eyes

---

6. Reed, *Preparing Missionaries for Intercultural Communication*, 144.

or engaging in similar immoral activities is harmful to his spiritual life and marriage. It is not loving oneself. The best way to love oneself is to train himself to live by biblical principles.

WORLDVIEW AND CROSS-CULTURAL GOSPEL COMMUNICATION

Communication is an integral element of missionary effectiveness. Communication is a vital tool for the ministry of preachers. It is through communication channels that missionaries intend to make disciples in foreign cultures. This task requires cross-cultural training, especially in the area of communication. It involves both verbal and non-verbal communication.

Cross-Cultural Sensitivity

Cross-cultural sensitivity needs to be valued if a missionary wants his life to integrate into loving foreign brothers. A breach of etiquette only adds frustration to the communication channel. Burping after a meal is considered impolite in America while it may be a sign of satisfaction and appreciation in China. Taking off shoes before entering someone's house may be a matter of cross-cultural sensitivity. Had a culture changed, the same action and same situation may stipulate different responses. Observing other people's behaviors is a key. If one is still not sure, he can always ask before the action and stay sensitive with cultural differences lest he may offend others unnecessarily. Christ embraced the Jewish culture in the days of his flesh. Cherishing and cultivating Christ's worldview should help us grow in our sensitivity and consideration toward other brothers and sisters in cross-cultural contexts.

Cross-Cultural Expression

The dominant worldview of the culture silhouettes its cultural expressions. That is why even expressions differ from culture to culture. In a competitive environment of highly populated cities, it is to be "excused" while walking on the street and bumping into someone by mistake. Most people do not even pay attention to it, and some may express their discomfort by briefly glaring at the other person and just pass by. Or some will rather use a phrase like, "A moment, please. Let me pass." That pretty much covers the whole situation.

An apology is rarely required. However, in a more relaxed environment of less populated regions, it becomes a different story. Proper expression of sorriness is normally expected even for a slight touch while passing on the street. Saying "Excuse me" or "Pardon me" becomes a cultural norm. Worldviews contour cultural expressions.

Noise in the Cross-Cultural Communication

In communications, noise can come from anything that prevents the sender's message from being correctly conveyed to the receiver. In cross-cultural communications, such noise can multiply and disturb a clear transmission of the foreign sender's message. To name a few forms of major cross-cultural communication noise, there are:

- Expression of emotions
- Perception of time
- Customs

Some cultures do not easily portray certain emotions in their social norms. Some of them do not even have a vocabulary for particular emotions in their native language. An outward expression of anger is almost a taboo for Thai while it is acceptable in the American culture. Generally, a smile in meetings is not encouraged in many African and Asian cultures. It can be misinterpreted as belittlement or silliness. Most Americans expect people to show up before the meeting time agreed upon. For many Africans, especially those who live in rural areas, the perception of time runs differently from Westerners. An event orientation shapes most of their livelihood rather than time orientation. American 10:00 a.m. does not necessarily mean African 10:00 a.m. It is not even about civilization but just a matter of different cultural understanding. It may be hard for people to read the facial expression of a Muslim woman who wears the "niqab" (Islamic female head covering) in public places. Misunderstanding can easily slip into communication because of such different customs. Without Christ's worldview incubated in our heart to enable us to embrace unfamiliar national customs, it can also be one disturbing form of noise in cross-cultural communication.

Biblical Principles of Cross-Cultural Gospel Communication

The Great Commission is about us going to the other culture, rather than bringing the other culture to us. Therefore, more effort is required for gospel workers to *learn* the other culture. It isn't primarily about people of the other culture getting influenced by the missionary's culture except those of biblical origins. Jesus' command is straightforward: ". . . *go* and make disciples of all nations . . ." It should be noted that he didn't exactly say, ". . . *bring* all nations and make disciples of them . . ." This explains why many elites who were brought from the Two-Thirds World to U.S.-based seminaries in the past for sponsored theological training haven't returned to their home countries after graduation but settled in the U.S.

A relationship is central to understanding cross-cultural discipleship. A disciple (μαθητής or *mathetes* in Greek) is an apprentice who stays closely with the teacher and accompanies him. For cross-cultural discipleship multiplication to occur, anything that cannot be self-replicated should not be imposed nor demonstrated for locals to imitate. Such things will easily evaporate when the missionary leaves the field later.

Also, when offering a confrontation or giving a rebuke to a disciple in cross-cultural contexts, it must be done in a mannerly and respectful way. If a missionary serves in an honor-shame cultural zone, shame should not be imposed in the disciplinary process. The local disciples' honor and face-saving must be considered even in exhortation. In an innocence-guilt culture, a local disciple's integrity in the gospel of grace must be upheld instead of entailing guilty feelings afterward. Stressing God's unchanging love and his preserved identity in Christ will be of merit when exhorting a disciple in a power-fear culture. Indeed, the worldview matters in making disciples in cross-cultural contexts. Embracing various worldviews while cultivating deeper in Christ's worldview will certainly enlarge our capacity to appreciate and make disciples of all nations more prudently. Indeed, that is Christ's command.

DISCUSSION AND REFLECTION QUESTIONS

1. It is practically unfeasible to put the three-dimensional round world accurately into two-dimensional flat maps. With that in mind, how do you respond to the Bible's claim of Jerusalem being the center of the nations (Ezekiel 5:5)?

2. The Bible sets the canon (standard) for every Christian practice. Take some time to reflect on why you do what you do as a Christian. For example, why do you go to church on Sunday? Why do you read and meditate on the Bible? The list goes on. Ask yourself what the rationale of your actions is. Do you pray because the Bible tells you to pray or

because someone else told you to pray? Do you close your eyes when you pray because the Bible tells you to do so or because you've seen someone else do so? This practice will help you distinguish a fine line between the Bible and culture.

3. Have you ever encountered any cross-cultural misunderstanding or miscommunication in the past? You meant one thing but the other person understood it as another, or vice versa. If yes, what could you have done differently?

9

Contextualization Is at Hand

The Lord Jesus has commanded us, his church, to go "into" all the world and preach the gospel to every creature (Mark 16:15). The task of going effectively *into* our world demands a skillful contextualization of all our efforts to transmit God's truths regardless of culture and generation. Jesus not only gave us the eminent mandate but also empirically demonstrated to us the perfect modes of contextualization through his incarnation. I wish to articulate and suggest some of the contextualization methodologies that may serve as a guideline for cross-cultural missionary outreach of the body of Christ from the missiological perspective.

WHY CONTEXTUALIZATION?

George Hunter once described contextualization as a task to "rewrap" the gospel in the clothing of their culture, to convey it in a vessel that will transport the gospel meaning to them.[1] Paul Hiebert's classic article entitled "Critical Contextualization" offers much help for missionaries. His critical contextualization model involves three steps. Step one is to "study the local culture phenomenologically." He insists that "the local church leaders and the missionary lead the congregation in uncritically gathering and analyzing the traditional beliefs, and customs associated with some question at hand." Step two requires exegesis of Scripture. In this second step, "the pastor or missionary leads the church in a study of the scriptures related to the question at hand." Step three involves a critical response, requiring

---

1. See Hunter, *To Spread the Power*, 158.

"the people corporately to evaluate critically their own past customs in the light of their new biblical understandings."[2] The unpeeling process of the culture with the probe of a biblical lens is recommended for the primary stage of contextualization. That is why a missionary must know the Bible inside out and also be conversant with the historical perspective (i.e., origin, development, or mutation) of the particular cultural element. After that, the repackaging process should be applied to what the biblical lens has reflected to be a link to the gospel intact. A new package with relevant cultural wrapping should be created.

Need of Contextualization

Some young preachers and Christian leaders may think that contextualization is about adopting new tech gadgets in their gospel presentations to reach out stylishly to the postmodern generation and Millennials, but contextualization essentially goes far deeper than that. Think about this. If 70 percent of the world's population doesn't get its information through literacy, could it be that the methods we're using to reach them with the gospel need to be reconsidered? Russell West illustrates why it's important to reach oral cultures through oral methods, and to work on enhancing the qualities already present in the leaders of our churches and communities.[3] God employed the most basic principle of effective communication, which was receptor-oriented communication.[4] This is the essence of contextualization.

Should an adequate contextualization take place, the transmission of the message should not be forced in haste. I constantly advise my students at IGSL and other seminaries to try not to cause abrupt changes in their churches and organizations unless they're in crisis. Even in organizational settings, sound contextualization is direly needed. I remember a story of one wise minister who was just transferred to his new pastoral assignment at a certain old church. Established decades before, the church had a pulpit positioned off to the side on the platform. The new pastor preferred to move it to the center to recode the culture of the church to be more seeker friendly and asked the elders if it'd be okay to do so. Most elders became violently dissident toward the idea, asserting that it was against the church tradition. Instead of quarreling about the non-essential issue, the pastor decided to concentrate on the essential issues and kept on preaching God's

---

2. Hiebert, "Critical Contextualization," 109.
3. West, "Re-Eventing of Theological Education."
4. Kraft, *Communicating the Gospel*, 17.

Word faithfully to his congregation. At the same time, the pastor stepped into a platform every Saturday night when no one was around and moved the pulpit toward the middle only half an inch at a time. Nobody in the congregation noticed the difference, including the elders. Nearly four years passed by, and guess where the pulpit was positioned by then? Exactly right in the middle of the platform where the pastor wanted, and no one in the congregation noticed the change because it was made so slowly and gradually. Moreover, no countercultural friction was caused in the process.

Wisdom, patience, and perseverance are pivotal in contextual applications. The Lord used Martin Luther to facilitate the Reformation because Luther was aware of how to draw the attention of people in his circle of influence, having priorly stayed in the Catholic Church. He was familiar with the rites of passage in the Catholic Church because he was a Catholic priest himself. He was capable of contextualizing his message for people who were sick and tired of the Catholic Church's corruption. Even Moses was able to minister adequately to Pharaoh because he knew the structure and passage of the Egyptian palace, having grown up as a prince. He knew exactly how to contextualize his message to the Egyptian rulers of his time. God's cross-cultural agents must know how to recode their messages in the way their target culture understands.

Any ministry deficient in sound contextualization can result in the unbalanced transmission of the gospel, which fails to integrate effectively into the "real" world. Some societies are more apt to conformity by culture, and it may be more accessible for a contextual leader to lead (or mislead) people in multitude. In such cases, it ought to be a responsibility of church leadership to take advantage of those societal characteristics and reroute their congregation to godly vogue in their attempt to articulate it and find an alternative way forward. Should they fail to engage in this integrative endeavor of faith and vogue, the ungodliness can take the form of a social norm. The local church may then lose spiritual authenticity, and her missionary effort is weakened. This is a critical reality.

Greatest Model of Contextualization, Christ

I'd like to present our Lord Jesus as the greatest model of contextualization. When the Messiah came into this world, the Wonderful Counselor, Mighty God, Everlasting Father, and Prince of Peace (Isaiah 9:6) deliberately chose to be born as a frail babe. Born as the Lamb of God who takes away the sin of the world (John 1:29), Jesus could have chosen an easier and quicker path to his vicarious death for the salvation of mankind. He, however, tarried at least thirty years, possibly 90 percent of his earthly incarnate life. From a missiologist's point of view, I tend to look at the period as Jesus' time of personal contextualization to the Jewish culture. Our Lord became a perfect Jew. Interestingly, his time of public ministry was relatively shorter—a little over three years. Jesus possibly spent 10 percent of the days of his flesh on earth with a specific agenda. He steered his public ministry to raise a small group of disciples who would become the seed of his church. Again, he could have directly headed to Calvary to fulfill his earthly mission instead of tarrying another several years. I see this duration as his contextualization period to his disciples.[5]

Jesus must have known what he was doing. His tarrying contextualization process on earth was initiated by his deep love for people—love for Jews, love for his disciples, and love for mankind, including you and me. Following Christ's model, contextualization of all aspects of our ministry expressions is at hand to reach "our" world. It was by Christ's love for us that he was willing to go through necessary contextualization through his incarnational lifestyle while on earth so that we may grasp his message. If you love Jesus, you will strive to contextualize his message in every area for a more effective delivery of it.

CROSS-CULTURAL GOSPEL PROPAGANDA

Importance of the Canon in Disciple-Making

Numbers and Deuteronomy show us the importance of the canon (standard). They do so more loudly than the New Testament because those books present the principles while the New Testament subsequently explains about applications of those principles. Some people approach and comprehend disciple-making from a human perspective, mainly because the canon has been neglected. Nevertheless, the standard should not be forgotten. Just as the two witnesses were "sent" to hostile and unresponsive audiences as described in Revelation 11:1–14, discipleship isn't about number or quantity but about attitude and quality. Biblical discipleship is not about pleasing and absorbing the majority. Even the two witnesses had more people who were "disturbed" by their message. However, they "went" to the people and prophesied in the language of the people. This fact confirms that true discipleship is about guiding people to follow the canon, not the discipler. You cannot make everybody a disciple. Still, you should concentrate on delivering a clear message of the canon and transmitting it to people.

5. Lee, *Missionary Candidate Training*, 79.

Sharing of the good news to everyone both near and far that Jesus Christ is the Son of God and that he fulfills the role of the Jewish Messiah and the Savior of the world takes on a natural process of multiplication. As Piper indicated, this is the supremacy of every missionary venture in history which ultimately brings glory to God.[6] Christian discipleship can propagate everywhere, even in cross-cultural contexts, just because the canon works in every individual life. Luke used the term "the Way" multiple times in his writings to describe this canon (Acts 9:2; 18:25; 18:26; 19:9; 22:4; 24:14; 24:22). Revelation 14:12 terms this canon as "the commandments of God":

> Here is the patience of the saints: here are they that keep *the commandments of God*, and the faith of Jesus.

The commandments of God, which has been translated from ἐντολή or *entole* in Greek, literally means "an authoritative prescription" (that is relevant in all cultural anthropology dimensions). This prescription is comprehensible and applicable for every age and setting. Discipleship, both in monocultural and cross-cultural contexts, is similar to rearing a child. Care, protection, hygiene, provision, education, and many other things are necessary to bring up a child to grow and mature to be a responsible adult. Everything supports and exists for the purpose of making a holistic person at last. The same goes for the disciple-making process. The prevailing grace of the Lord, the great care and sacrifice of a mentor, and the faithful commitment and teachable ear of a disciple work together to produce a mature man and woman of God. On the same note, it was observed that the spiritually new and young converts found our discipleship program more receptive and naturally rooted in their hearts, compared with people who were previously groomed elsewhere. Even a parable narrated by our Lord in Luke 5:36–39 confirms this phenomenon: "And no one after drinking old wine wants the new, for they say, 'The old is better'" (Luke 5:39).

Cultural Conflicts

Missionaries are known as the pronouns of cross-cultural workers. However, it was said that even missionaries are identified as feeling most comfortable on the airplane—that is, between cultures. Cross-cultural discipleship is right at the core of the Great Commission. Successful cross-cultural workers in any sector see the need to facilitate their propaganda through the identification process with the locals.

---

6. See Piper, *Let the Nations Be Glad!*, 51.

Cultural conflicts have been serious in history. All wars in history, small and large, have been clashes between cultures (i.e., couples, companies, churches, organizations, societies, countries, etc.). For example, American tourists in Paris often regard French waiters as rude because of their brusque behavior and their lack of helpfulness. Because waiters in the United States generally seem to be friendly and helpful, these tourists expect all waiters to behave similarly.[7] When they do not, their behavior is interpreted as rude. Instead, the pattern of doing a minimal amount is merely a reflection of a French cultural norm of individualism—take care of yourself and expect others to take care of themselves—a norm particularly likely to operate in the urban environment of Paris. The behavior is, in fact, relatively unmotivated, but the American, attributing more to the behavior pattern than is actually there, interprets it as an intent to be rude or to put down the tourist.[8]

The standard should be stipulated to overcome cultural clashes. The standard of biblical guidelines for being cross-cultural is authoritative, otherwise war and conquest may inevitably emerge. In that case, people are liable to take a destructive methodology for being cross-cultural. Genuine cross-cultural effort is possible and natural only through the biblical approach. All other methodologies exhibit superiorism of one culture over the other.[9]

Even the reason many local pastors fail to see penetrating influence in their multifaceted, multiracial, and multicultural city is that they fail to think cross-culturally. Therefore, a cross-cultural approach and adjustment for Christian discipleship are unavoidable for anyone in Christian ministry, let alone anyone who is involved in working in a multicultural or cross-cultural setting. Cross-cultural discipleship applies to all areas, including even youth ministry to teenagers and young adults, transcending and getting into their culture. It is about all areas of cultures, not just mission field cultures.

CONTEXTUALIZATION AS GOD'S WAY FOR REACHING THE WORLD

One day I was told a humorous joke as I was about to officiate the wedding of one of my church members back in Kenya. A certain pastor officiated the wedding ceremony of a couple. This grateful couple sent a present to the

---

7. See Matsumoto, *Cultural Influences on Research Methods and Statistics.*
8. See Schein, *Organizational Culture and Leadership.*
9. For more discussions on the need of standard for every culture, see Fortosis, "Model for Understanding Cross-Cultural Morality."

pastor to appreciate him, and he replied to them with a "thank you" card. In his card, he intended to remind them to read Philippians 4:18 and show how refreshing their present was to him.

> I have received full payment and have more than enough. I am amply supplied, now that I have received from Epaphroditus the gifts you sent. They are a fragrant offering, an acceptable sacrifice, pleasing to God.

Nonetheless, exhausted after a heavy weekend schedule, the pastor mistakenly wrote John 4:18, not Philippians 4:18, on the card. Lo and behold! Imagine the shock and wonder the couple must have felt when they took a Bible and read John 4:18.

> The fact is, you have had five husbands, and the man you now have is not your husband. What you have just said is quite true.

A mistake of just one word on the pastor's card to the newlyweds changed the whole meaning of his message. In contextualization, both preservations of meaning and flexibility of function ought to be upheld in balance. A small mistake either in exegeting Scripture biblically or suggesting culturally functional applications can change its entire message to the target culture. A tiny mistake, for now, may leave a lasting grave impact on the Christianity of that group for generations.

Suppose you have a hole on brick pavement and you wish to replace it with another brick but you don't have the exact shape and size. Many times, that is the case of cultural contextualization. When you must translate something but can't find the right word in the target culture, the experience finds a similar dilemma and requires tolerable contextualization. It is because the way people of one culture reason isn't the same with the way people of another culture reason. That is why cultural humor does not apply everywhere. What is found appealing in one culture may not be as appealing in other cultures, unless, of course, it is a universal one, which is seldom found.[10] This factor adds on the list of why careful and appropriate contextualization is at hand for effective cross-cultural gospel work.

For example, John describes in his Gospel, initially addressed to Jews and some Gentiles, how Jesus Christ demonstrated the perfect tabernacle, the meeting place of God and men. The original Greek text of John 1:14 reads:

> καὶ ὁ λόγος σὰρξ ἐγένετο καὶ ἐσκήνωσεν ἐν ἡμῖν, καὶ ἐθεασάμε θα τὴν δόξαν αὐτοῦ, δόξαν ὡς μονογενοῦς παρὰ πατρός, πλήρ ης χάριτος καὶ ἀληθείας. (Tyndale House Greek New Testament)

However, the New International Version landed up in the following translation:

> The Word became flesh and *made his dwelling* among us. We have seen his glory, the glory of the one and only Son, who came from the Father, full of grace and truth.

The Greek vocabulary ἐσκήνωσεν (*eskenosen*) literally means "tabernacled." Upon reading this verse, Jewish readers would picture Jesus representing the meeting place of God and men because their culture historically evolved from the tabernacle of the Old Testament. Yet, most English Bible translations are suited with such contextual translations as "made his dwelling," "made his home," and "dwelt" because that would be more comprehensive to most non-Jewish readers. Modes of contextualization are closely knit with an embodiment of linguistic and customary understanding from an anthropological perspective, incarnational approach in a missiological perspective, and integrative thinking from a sociological perspective.

CONTEXTUALIZATION AS OUR WAY FOR REACHING THE WORLD

Many missionary anthropologists have written on the subject of contextualization upon the conceptualization of the term in 1972.[11] Under the theme of "dynamic equivalence churches," ongoing effort to make the

---

10. Keller, *Center Church*, 95–96.
11. Theological Education Fund, *Ministry in Context*, 28; Bosch, *Transforming Mission*, 420–32.

embodiment of God's Word culturally relevant to the target audience within the biblical guidelines has been made.¹²

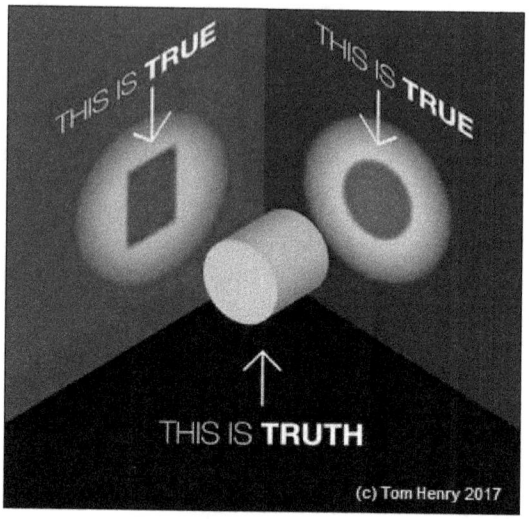

As God's messengers, we're trying to present God's Word, a totality of God's truth, to the world. However, we all have different cultural backgrounds and understandings, and therefore tend to look at the truth from different angles. It may be perceived true to me in my own culture but it may not be so in other cultures. The truth we bring *into* other cultures must look likewise true to them.¹³ For instance, what portrays as true to Africans may not be necessarily true to Asians. What portrayed to be true to the Baby Boomers may not exactly appeal to be true to Generation Z. How you need to present it to a given culture demands proper cross-cultural contextualization. The English prefix "con-" connotes the meaning of "together" or "with." Contextualization seeks to articulate the use of the text of God's Word in the light of different cultures so that recipients may understand it relevantly and perceive God's message.

> Biblically faithful (Meaning)
> + Culturally sensitive (Function)
> ―――――――――――――――――
> = Contextualization

---

12. See Kraft, *Christianity in Culture*.
13. Henry, "It's All a Matter of Perspective."

Jackson Wu states that contextualization helps us minister with a biblically faithful and culturally meaningful message and methods.[14] The adequate interpretation of the biblical truths in the contexts of time and setting leads to contextualization, not syncretism. Under-contextualization may lead to the syncretism of tradition (separatism). Over-contextualization may bring about syncretism of culture (accommodation). Only healthy contextualization can result in a missional engagement (transformation).[15]

Also, it should not be overlooked that a cross-cultural gospel worker can get influenced by ungodly cultures of the target group instead of influencing it with godly cultures. Thus, one must stay constantly vigilant to look after his own spiritual status and relationship with the Lord before applying contextualization in the field. On the other hand, extractionistic approaches to missions may require a high degree of indoctrination and a long period of dependence on the missionary because the frame of reference is too foreign to the national believers. This is good for controlling the message, but it hardly allows contextualization in the target group and culture.[16] We don't want to do this either. The contextual implementation of our message can catalyze explosive indigenous growth.[17]

CONTEXTUALIZATION ISN'T HARD

Our message has to be contextualized so that it may go *into* all the world for effective transmission. My research affirms that three things need to be considered for holistic contextualization. One needs to be mindful about:

- Home culture (My culture)
- Field culture (Their culture)
- Bible (Biblical guideline)

---

14. Wu, *One Gospel for All Nations*, ch. 3.
15. Moreau, "Contextualization."
16. Gration, "Conversion in Cultural Context."
17. See Handy, "Correlating the Nevius Method."

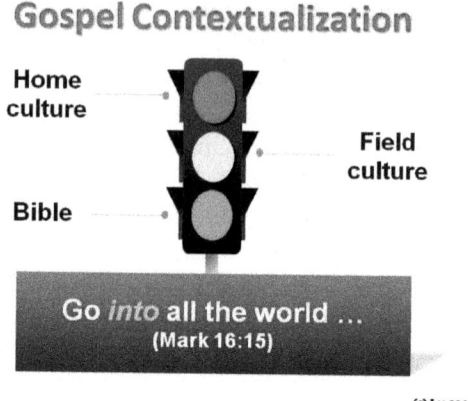

Sound contextualization begins with cognitive comprehension of why they do what they do and attempt to put oneself in particular cultural shoes. It should develop into a projection of that comprehension; it is more than sharing common attire, food, and language, although they may greatly contribute to forming cross-cultural comprehension. Failures to be cross-cultural can lead gospel workers to an unbalanced lifestyle and even depression.

Many preachers I met in Africa expressed their preference to wear a collared robe while ministering in pastoral ceremonies. They tend to believe that a collared robe bestowed on their performance a sense of authenticity. Authenticity does not originate from the robe. It comes from the preacher's walk with the Lord who called him. Church history in England tells us that a collared robe originated from an idea of keeping the minister's voice box warm from the intense cold of the English winter. It had little to do with the minister's authenticity or spirituality. You have to know why you're doing what you're doing for sound contextualization.

The example of Jesus' disciples beginning to anoint with oil when healing the sick (Mark 6:13; James 5:14) demonstrates a process of contextualization. As far as the biblical records are mentioned, Jesus never anointed anyone with oil when he was healing the sick. However, since it was culturally adaptable and contemporarily acceptable, the practice was implanted over the process. The Jewish community was familiar with anointing oil even from the Old Testament period. This is another classic implication of the principle of "similar kind, less friction," which I introduced earlier in this book. Another example is found in Matthew 17:27.

But so that we may not offend them, go to the lake and throw out your line. Take the first fish you catch; open its mouth and you will find a four-drachma coin. Take it and give it to them for my tax and yours.

Even the King of the universe wasn't always challenging the existing culture unless it was evil. If there was someone who did not need to pay tax, it must have been Jesus, the Creator of this world who doesn't owe anything to anybody. But he did. It guides us with what to tolerate and what to tackle in our contextualization efforts. Correct contextualization should lead us to keep *meaning* and navigate *function*. It may vary from person to person and from culture to culture. The world is in high demand for biblically sound contextualizers of the message.

At IGSL where I teach, there is a three-week practicum course required for all master's level students. Students comprised of various countries are mobilized into multiple teams to go cooperate with local churches and ministries every summer. Lodging, planning, and ministering together for three weeks as a team often reveals their hidden personalities, and interpersonal conflicts intermittently rouse out of frustrating cross-cultural communications. To give practical examples, a Nepalese student may nod his head side to side (meaning "yes") during discussions and other teammates may comprehend his response as "no." Filipino students, who are mostly non-confrontational, have many indirect ways to say "no" without actually saying "no" in conversations, and this can confuse other teammates. A Burundian student serving food with his left hand may be annoying to an Indian teammate. Korean teammates prefer to take off their shoes inside of a house while other nationalities enter it with their shoes on. My experience with IGSL students suggests that cultural implication matters a great deal in the real world. One says something but the other may understand it quite differently from the conveyor's intention. Cultural reflections do refract the original message and create new implications. Such a missiological principle ought to be contemplated in the contextualization process.

The cultural study covers a wide spectrum from a racial and provincial dimension to an individual dimension. In this context, contextualization is an attempt to live together with others, even with those individuals who are of different and various cultural backgrounds. Contextualization then assumes that the pure gospel must be presented in a package that is most culturally general to the community.[18]

---

18. Rodewald, "Barriers to the Gospel."

Case #1—Early Rise Service in the Church of Korea

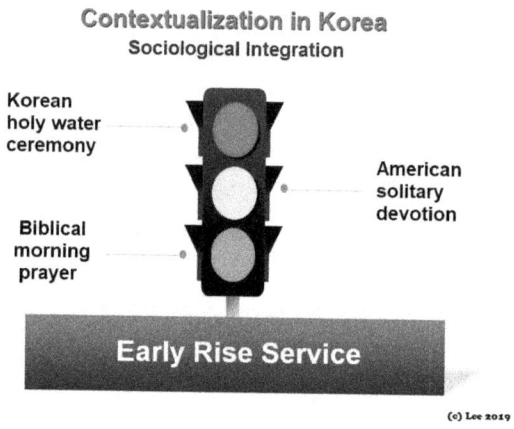

When the early American missionaries were sent to Korea, they only had minimal success in the beginning due to failure to culturally contextualize their message. Koreans were suffering from political conflicts with Japan and surrounding countries, thus vigilance toward foreigners was high. It took their patience first to earn trust from the royal palace and general public alike. Even after establishing a bonding relationship with Korean believers, they had to continuously deal with some social issues that were deeply related to Buddhism, Confucianism, and shamanism. One of the rampant practices was a shamanistic ritual called the holy water ceremony at dawn. Many mothers would fetch a bowl of clean water and pray to the gods of heaven and earth for the well-wishing of their family members. Even some Korean believers did not get rid of this ungodly practice after they were converted to Christ. When American missionaries witnessed this common tradition of the holy water ceremony in Korean households, they knew they'd need to come up with adequate contextualization to deal with the impending social phenomenon.

I'd like to draw your attention here to reflect (1) the Korean field culture, (2) the missionary's home culture, and finally (3) what the Bible has to say about early rise service. Jesus prayed early in the morning (Mark 1:35). The psalmist began his day with prayer in the morning (Psalms 5:3; 63:1, KJV). The Bible confirms that it is scripturally sound to pray in the morning.

Oral lore tells us that some missionaries wittily sought to replace the holy water ceremony with a godly practice instead of bluntly abolishing it.

With the support of Korean national church leaders, they introduced an alternative church meeting at dawn and encouraged the believers to come and pray to the Lord instead of the gods of heaven and earth.[19] A study shows that most American Christians prefer to pray solo and silent at their homes,[20] and it wasn't exactly compatible with American culture to gather people every day at dawn at church facilities. Nevertheless, they made an effort to contextualize this Korean dawn culture into something that might be biblically faithful and culturally relevant. They succeeded in decoding the ungodly ceremony and recoding it with the creation of a godly cultural norm rather than imposing a common American prayer style on Koreans.

Today, the church of Korea is known for her zeal to corporately seek the Lord in early mornings. This contextualization effort was ultimately brought to fruition when thousands of believers continued to flock into local church facilities to attend early-rise services every day and to pray for their family members' well-wishing. Generations have passed by from this possible inception of a Korean early-rise service. While it is praiseworthy to see many Korean Christians still seeking to start their days with the Lord by attending early rise services, it should not be undermined that only a fraction of them remain after the service to spend time alone with the Lord in personal prayer. Just participating in the service makes the majority of attendees feel somewhat content to the point that the biblical intention of morning prayer gets ignored. The point of morning prayer is to individually seek God's face to commune and be filled with the Holy Spirit so that one may live a life of submission to God's will for the rest of the day. The intention of the contextualization was well meant, however, we can't neglect to examine both the pros and cons of its application after generations have passed by. This is why it is vitally important for Christians to consider why we do what we do in all our Christian practices.

Case #2—Property Dedication in the Church of the Philippines

Having taught and coached for years scores of students at IGSL on pastoral ceremonial responsibilities, some unbiblical elements were discovered in performing their ministerial duties of property dedication. Property dedication is a common religious practice in many cultures, both Christian and non-Christian. Wishing for the divine bestowment of protection and prosperity may be a natural desire for anyone who acquires new property, from a car to a house.

19. Lee and Lee, *Introduction to Missiology*, 229–30.
20. Barna Group, "Silent and Solo."

However, some have gone astray to emphasize wishing for divine protection even to the point of unbiblical fortune-seeking and incantatory behaviors. Again, let us reflect on (1) the Filipino field culture, (2) the missionary's home culture, and finally (3) what the Bible has to say about property dedication. Certain superstitious beliefs existed before Christianity was introduced to the Philippines. People in rural areas would sacrifice a white chicken to sprinkle its blood on the corners of their property in hope that that they would be protected from misfortunes and haul in lucks. Some would put coins on the cornerstone of their house for protection from earthquakes and other natural calamities.[21] Carelessly replacing or mixing such pagan practices with the biblical concept of dedication can be dangerously misleading, regardless of the dedicator's sincerity.

I've witnessed some Filipino ministers applying anointing oil on the property during the ceremony. Although there're only a few occasions in the Bible when the anointing oil was applied on property, this practice may still be acceptable within the biblical parameters because we find similar occasions in the Bible several times. Jacob anointed a pillar at Bethel while making a vow to the Lord (Genesis 31:13). Moses anointed the pieces of equipment in the tabernacle with oil (Exodus 30:26–28). Israeli soldiers were instructed to put oil on their shields in preparation for war (Isaiah

---

21. "Do you Want to Bless your Home?"

21:5). Even though I've never seen anyone anointing property with oil for dedication back in the United States or South Korea, it should not be prohibited, in accordance with the principle we earlier discussed.

Most church members in the Philippines prefer for their ministers to come and do the blessing. Hence, a minister must remind the dedicator about the biblical basis of why they do what they do in the dedication ceremony. The biblical practice of property dedication is mainly to acknowledge Christ's lordship over the object. It should be a confession of remembrance (Deuteronomy 8:18) and thanksgiving (1 Chronicles 29:11–13) as well as acknowledgment of God's ownership (Psalm 24:1) and involvement (Psalm 127:1). Crystal-clear instruction may be in order to prohibit the dedicator's focus from landing on the anointing oil or any other object (or any other person). God should be the center of attention in the ceremony. This is more so in the Filipino culture, which has been heavily influenced by Catholic relic veneration.[22] Extra elements for personal creativity and cultural relevance can be still added to a program within the parameters of the biblical and cultural boundaries. Under the proper guidance of a minister and orientation of dedicator, a property dedication can be one exciting and blessed commemoration of God's goodness.

Having lived in different places and cultures, I learned that training myself to constantly think about what I would do in their cultural perspective usually helps me to enhance greater cultural homogenization. There're generally three questions to ask to generate the best contextualization:

- What would my culture do in this given situation?
- What would their culture do in this given situation?
- What would Jesus do in this given situation?

A missionary needs to thoroughly comprehend the local culture. He has to be mindful of why the local people do what they do. The more a missionary becomes localized and creates a closer bonding with the local people, the better contextualization is made out. In other words, the principle of "similar kind, less friction" pays off even in the contextualization process. National church leaders are often in a better position to come up with a contextualized method for ungodly or evil traditions. If a missionary can prayerfully suggest and seek to replace such customs with godly (or at least not ungodly) practice, that will be a way forward. He should know where to draw the line between ungodliness, godliness, and neutrality. The collaboration of foreign missionaries and local Christian leaders to think

22. Song, "Contextualization and Discipleship."

through on this subject will produce a more biblically based and culturally suitable substitute. The gradual process of decoding the ungodly culture and recoding it with godly culture is not only expected but also possible in cross-cultural ministry. Tireless inquiry and research will bear the fruit of timely enlightenment as the Holy Spirit, the mastermind of world mission, provides direction and wisdom.

DISCUSSION AND REFLECTION QUESTIONS

1. Why is contextualization necessary in ministry, especially in cross-cultural contexts? Explain in your own words.

2. Jackson Wu speaks of the contextualization that helps us come up with a biblically faithful and culturally meaningful message and methods. How would his statement affect your understanding and practice of cross-cultural contextualization?

3. Lee states that one has to be conversant with his home culture, field culture, and the Bible to generate sound cross-cultural contextualization. Select any ungodly culture of the mission field that you're engaged in and see if you can articulate each component. Check if you can apply the contextualization principle given in this chapter to that particular culture.

PART IV

Desire of the Nations

10

Cultural Homogenization and Incarnation

> And I will shake all nations, and the *desire of all nations* shall come: and I will fill this house with glory, saith the Lord of hosts. (Haggai 2:7, KJV)

God's dream is to see all nations coming to him and to manifest his glory for the renewal of all things. For this holistic dream to come true, a cross-cultural gospel worker may need to get equipped with the issues elaborated in this chapter. During my six terms of missionary service in Africa and Asia, God has given me opportunities to fellowship with other missionaries and cross-cultural workers who had apparent success in their missionary works and disciple-making efforts. Several common traits that made them excel in their works were soon discovered. One of the most vivid characteristics discovered was that every one of them bore the marks of the incarnational lifestyle. Every fruit-bearing missionary had to go through extra miles to be localized while imitating Christ's lifestyle in perseverance. It was noticed that only then could they produce sound local disciples. Such an exemplary lifestyle produced local disciples converting and guiding other local people, thus making biblical multiplication of cross-cultural discipleship possible.

THE HOLISTIC APPROACH OF THE MISSIO DEI

Going cross-cultural should take place in three holistic dimensions, as 1 Thessalonians 5:23 implies compartmentalized dimensions of the *missio Dei*:

> May God himself, the God of peace, sanctify you through and through. May your whole [1] spirit, [2] soul and [3] body be kept blameless at the coming of our Lord Jesus Christ.

1. Spirit (spiritual aspect of the *missio Dei*): This integral area can be ministered through the incarnational life and gospel-centered work of a missionary. A missionary ought to pursue modeling his life after Christ and, consequently, both the missionary and local disciples would become mature, attaining to the whole measure of the fullness of Christ.

2. Soul (educational aspect of the *missio Dei*): This critical need can be met through teaching and educational ministry. Just as Puritans established schools alongside churches so that everyone would be able to read God's Word, a missionary should not neglect meeting the needs of the human soul and encouraging people to love God with their soul as well.

3. Body (physical aspect of the *missio Dei*): Orthopraxis through care, medical, and mercy ministries must be demonstrated on the field. Orthopraxis adds legs and feet to our biblical worldview. The biblical worldview resonates with *what* and orthopraxis with *how*. The public ministry of our Lord Jesus was evenly distributed for preaching, teaching, and *healing* people. This area completes the holistic approaches of the *missio Dei*.

Nevertheless, it came to my attention that the most difficult area for missionaries to live the incarnational lifestyle, especially those originating from First World countries, was adapting themselves to the local economy and standard of living of the Two-Thirds World, where the majority of mission fields are still found. If a missionary is assigned to a ministry setting where the economy median of the local people he works with is close to or higher than that of his home country, it shouldn't be much problem. Usually, it takes less effort to upgrade one's economy level than downgrade, provided adequate financial support.

It is quite a challenging issue, for instance, for an average middle-class American family of four that used to live on a $92,500 yearly budget[1] to

---

1. Amadeo, "What Is Considered Middle-Class Income?"

suddenly adapt to Kenya's urban middle-class standard of living of $4,800 a year.[2] A missionary's adaptability to the local economy and standard of living is a great challenge not only for the missionary himself but also for his family members. It may create devastation to the missionary family, who will likely face a downgrade of the standard of living rather than an upgrade. A single missionary may find it less burdensome yet likewise challenging for such a degree of economical downgrade. Missionaries usually end up choosing either one of two options that lie before them: either they choose to live in a "little homeside" environment or make burdensome efforts toward localization in this area. Though challenging, it is an unavoidable area where all the effective missionaries have strived to make efforts because this ultimately leads them to experience bonding, the first and foremost step toward the incarnational lifestyle, as clearly shown in the example of the best cross-cultural worker, our Lord Jesus Christ, who came to live as one of the Jews.

INCARNATION IS IN CRITICAL NEED

A doorstep of effective disciple-making effort in cross-cultural contexts is incarnation through the bonding procedure. Bonding opens the ultimate pathway to cross-cultural discipleship.[3] Therefore, missionaries should experience bonding in their effort to adapt to the local lifestyle as a means to exercise the incarnational ministry style.

One of the most widespread underlying worldviews that hinders incarnational bonding effort may be neocolonialism. That is, Westerners, who used to be "lording" it over other nations, may subconsciously consider foreign nationals of the Two-Thirds World as somewhat inferior to them, even in the spiritual dimension, and then treat them from a paternalistic view. Such unbiblical models of missionary life and work cripple the current mission enterprise. In the name of "efficient" mobility, some missionaries might drive a four-wheel-drive Jeep, which the local pastors he works with will probably never have a chance to drive in their lifetime. For a "protective" environment, some missionaries may stay and eat at a hotel while visiting local churches and their indigenous coworkers instead of sharing their local foods and lodgings to promote Christian brotherhood.

Some missionaries leave their mission fields after years of tenure with toil and moil without succeeding local disciples who will carry on their works. The local leaders may have never felt that the missionary was

2. Ilako, "Middle-Class Sinking in Debt."
3. Malina, *Cultural Anthropology and Christian Origins*, 69–74.

one of them, and perhaps the feeling could have been mutual even for the missionary. Where there was no bonding formed in relationship, trust and friendship were hardly created, thus discipleship may have rarely taken place. No matter what funding, building, and projects missionaries may leave behind upon their departure from the field, the instruction of Great Commission remains apparent with its sine qua non: ". . . Go and *make disciples . . .*" Should there be no reproduction of the local discipleship, the missionary work may have not been complete.[4]

Love of our brothers—whether they're the Shemites or Hamites or Japhetithes—will motivate our voluntary and willful cross-cultural identification, causing spiritual, educational, and physical homogeneity. Human history has been filled with stories of brother's assaulters rather than brother's keepers. Just as God reminded Cain after murdering Abel that he was called to be his brother's keeper, brothers and sisters in Christ are especially obliged to keep one another transcending cultures and borders. In this regard, Galatians 6:2 verifies that we're to "carry each other's burdens, and in this way, we will fulfill the law of Christ."

Christian brothers can, and should, live in harmony and experience homogeneity. It serves as a pathway to effective cross-cultural discipleship. Honest and open communication paves its first doorstep. Cross-cultural workers can find and connect a link to the introduction of the gospel and spiritual fellowship with any ethnic group on earth by understanding and applying this principle. Matthew 10:11–16 tells us:

> *Whatever town or village you enter, search there for some worthy person and stay at their house until you leave.* As you enter the home, give it your greeting. If the home is deserving, let your peace rest on it; if it is not, let your peace return to you. If anyone will not welcome you or listen to your words, leave that home or town and shake the dust off your feet . . . Therefore be as shrewd as snakes and as innocent as doves.

Jesus still reminds his missionaries today: "Whatever town or village you enter, search there for some worthy person and stay at their house until you leave." This concept was enabled by Jesus' belief that all people are brothers and sisters who originated from one family tree. It is natural for a brother to stay in his own brother's place when visiting him. Jesus' word still resonates down the centuries for those who are going into missions. It is therefore advised for a missionary to stay with a local church leader at his house unless one is ailing with a health issue and/or the host declines for any reason, inclusive of a security reason, etc. Some missionaries lodging in

---

4. See Hesselgrave, *Planting Churches Cross-Culturally*.

a luxurious hotel while going for a mission tour should seriously reconsider this biblical principle.

At the EAPTC missionary school, the candidates undergoing training drills are reminded to be mindful of too-frequent homeside visits, especially in their first term of a field assignment. Thanks to the globalization and advancement of technology, missionaries can now travel by flight to almost anywhere within a day or two. Yet, we shouldn't forget that before air travel was made available to the public a missionary would take months to get to their field by ship. A homeside visit was unlikely to happen within the first few years. There was no jetlag caused by time differences. Everyone would gradually adjust to different time zones as they traveled on a ship. It wasn't likely that they'd return home soon once they embarked for their cross-cultural mission overseas. Perhaps this factor additionally contributed toward the rationales behind active field adjustment and dynamic acculturation of old-time missionaries.

THE PERIL OF COLONIAL INFLUENCE

The problem is typically found wherever Christian mission work is carried out, especially where the mission work was influenced by colonialism or neocolonialism. Successful cross-cultural discipleship demands three suitable requirements: firstly, a suitable understanding of culture[5]; secondly, a suitable approach to the mission field; and thirdly, a suitable spiritual condition of the field. Neither an exclusivism-based receiver mode nor a colonialism-based giver mode will promote cross-cultural discipleship. Besides, the spiritual moldability of the mission field is another paramount prerequisite. It is noticeable that the attitudes of the missionary force that entered Korea with the gospel were distinct from the missionary force that entered Kenya in the same nineteenth century. While the Anglican Church or Church of England, closely associated with the British government, eventually propagandized colonization of Kenya and encouraged English (often Christian) naming of nationals, both Presbyterian and Methodist missionaries who came to Korea added Korean names for themselves for the purpose of local identification. Intentionally or unintentionally, while indigenous naming of early missionaries in Korea portrayed bonding endeavors to indigenous people, early missionaries to Kenya often portrayed superiority to indigenous people. Later, such a warm gesture of missionaries in Korea toward the incarnational lifestyle earned the great affection of the local people, in contrast to the Japanese' forceful name changes imposed

---

5. See Demarest and Matthews, *Dictionary of Everyday Theology and Culture*, 102–5.

on Koreans to Japanese names during colonization. Some European and North American missionaries who even stood with and comforted Koreans during the Japanese colonization and the Korean War period became role models of incarnational mission work to many Koreans until today. Cultural homogenization of a missionary's lifestyle on the mission field is a significant issue to consider for effective cross-cultural discipleship worldwide.

Cross-cultural workers should aim first to understand the people to whom they go to engage.[6] Understanding of the people to whom the workers go requires incarnational bonding,[7] as clearly shown in the example of Jesus, the Missionary from heaven to mankind, Jews, and the Twelve. It concerns the core value and effectiveness of cross-cultural discipleship.

Upon arrival on the mission field, missionaries ought to pursue the incarnational lifestyle in all areas, including the area of adaptation to the local economy and standard of living. Ideal, yet realistic approaches to adapting to the local economy and standard of living need both theological and missiological considerations. My research of many years supports this position, and I'd like to suggest three principles that uphold it.

THE KENOSIS PRINCIPLE

First of all, the kenosis principle affirms this position. A missionary's incarnational self-limitation is a great trait that resembles Christ's kenosis as shown in Philippians 2:7.[8] The Greek word κένωσις, or *kenosis*, which is translated as "made nothing" in our English Bibles, points to a voluntary act of self-abasement or self-limitation. This kenosis principle suggests the modest lifestyle of a missionary family on the field.

Should a missionary aspire to grow in cross-cultural dynamics, a constitutional transformation of his cultural DNA needs to take place to a certain extent. Having believed the inerrancy of the Scriptures as an evangelical Christian, the world must have sprung out of the homogeneity found in Noah's family after the flood. It even stretches to the pre-flood era and reaches up to Adam and eventually to God (Luke 3:38).

---

6. See Kraft, *Anthropology for Christian Witness*; Bell, *Gospel for Muslims*; ITAP International, "Culture in the Workplace Questionnaire Overview"; Schein, *Organizational Culture and Leadership*; Caligiuri and Tarique, "Predicting Effectiveness in Global Leadership Activities"; Jang, "Is the Life of Korean Missionaries Exemplary?"

7. Linford Stutzman, "Incarnational Approach to Mission."

8. See Langmead, *Word Made Flesh*."

Once a missionary begins to see that we all came from one giant family tree and that those foreign disciples are his long-lost relatives, it traces closer to the cultural homogeneity that existed at the very inception of history. That novel homogeneity relates to the concept of *imago Dei* ("image of God" in Latin). Second Corinthians 4:4 elaborates further on this: "... Christ, who is the *image* of God." Simply put, all humans are created after Christ. This is why a team of people from *all* nations can come to Christ, find the common denominator in Christ, and work together in Christ.

Christ, the mighty God (Isaiah 9:6), was even willing to identify himself with mere humans as their brother (Matthew 12:49; 28:10; John 20:17) and friend (John 15:15). Just as the King of the universe humbled himself to such an utmost extent, so can we adjust to other fellow brothers living in another culture. This motion substantially frames the foundation of the kenosis principle. Restoration of the *imago Dei* precedes the fulfillment of the *missio Dei*.

Among many examples, the book *Mission Legacies* speaks of Bruno Gutmann, a missionary to the Moshi people of East Africa, who humbly exercised great self-limitation and earned the local people's heart for the gospel.

> Gutmann was a dedicated missionary. I heard him remark on several occasions, not entirely without pride, "I have never been a parish pastor, but I am thankful that I have been able to remain a missionary all my life." Following the example of Saint Paul in 1 Corinthians 9:20, 22-23, he wanted to become a Mchagga (an accepted member of the Chagga tribe); and he was able to achieve it in a relatively short lifespan only because he dedicated himself so completely to the Moshi people. In this self-limitation—he did not even learn to speak Kiswahili well— lies the root of his greatness. Precisely because of his intensive involvement in a single tribe in East Africa, he was able to understand and love them as no other European did.[9]

The kenosis principle affirms that missionaries should experience bonding in their effort to adapt to the local lifestyle as a mean to exercise the incarnational ministry style.

---

9. Anderson et al., *Mission Legacies*, 179.

THE ADJUSTMENT PRINCIPLE

Secondly, the adjustment principle argues for bonding in their effort to adapt to the local lifestyle as a means to exercise the incarnational ministry style. To create crucial incarnational bonding, a missionary should make efforts to adjust his standard of living to that of locals he wishes to reach. For this purpose, in some mission organizations newcomer missionaries are encouraged to: (1) be willing to live with a local family, (2) limit personal belongings to forty-four pounds (twenty kilos), (3) use only local public transportation, and (4) expect to carry out language learning in the context of relationships that the learner is responsible to develop and maintain.[10] When all is said and done, it is an undeniable fact that the greatest single focal point of tension today between the sending mission and the receiving church is related to money.[11] Therefore, missionaries can model for indigenous staff a modest lifestyle that reflects godly financial stewardship.[12] It is a general rule that missionaries should live at the level of the people they want to reach.[13]

My research attempted to serve as a contemporary paradigm of cross-cultural Christian work. It was a God-led privilege for me to make this research after my sixteen years of experience as a career missionary in Kenya and Africa at large to add a taste on the practical side. Also, my life has been based in Asia, America, and Africa in almost equal proportions while it was largely consumed by making disciples in those world regions, mostly in cross-cultural settings. Jesus' incarnation principle has been attested to work globally because it has been tested, facilitated, and proven effective from old to modern times. Paul became a Gentile, Jew, and barbarian and to reach all of them (1 Corinthians 9:20–22). He refers to the principle of cross-cultural homogenization. Genuine cross-cultural homogenization is "*cross*"-cultural homogenization. Christ willingly carried the cross for our sins and reached out to us with his sacrificial love. His cross love still motivates a missionary to voluntarily cross over cultures and economic standards to reach the lost. The adjustment principle affirms that missionaries should experience the bonding in their effort to adapt to the local lifestyle as a means to exercise the incarnate ministry style.

---

10. Brewster and Brewster, *Language Exploration*.
11. See Kane, *Understanding Christian Missions*.
12. See Weightman, "Essential Components."; Dayton, *Mission Handbook*.
13. See Weightman, "Essential Components"; Blackaby and Blackaby, *Spiritual Leadership*.

THE HEART PRINCIPLE

The third reason to believe that missionaries should experience bonding in their effort to adapt to the local lifestyle as a means to exercise the incarnational ministry style is related to the heart principle. It is important for the nationals whom a missionary works with to notice his heartfelt effort to identify with them in all areas, including the financial area. Kane's perspective on identification with local economy standards suggests a realistic way forward when the gap between the missionary and the national workers is usually so great.[14] A missionary must make a sincere attempt to reasonably downgrade his living standard to show his willingness to identify with the people he came to serve. This gesture may be more penetrative in countries where an anti-neocolonialism, anti-Western sentiment, and anti-Christian mindset are latent in people's way of thinking.[15] Contextualization begins with humility. A downgrade also needs and begins with humility.[16] However, bonding and "going native" are not the same thing.[17] The goal is to become incarnational (which is the model of Jesus coming to live among us). Obviously, no human missionary can achieve the level of incarnation the Son of God demonstrated by being born as a man. There is undeniably a difference between Christ's incarnation and our incarnation. Ours only aims to reach a bicultural status where a missionary is "together-in-difference" with the locals.[18] This may be stressful, but, in the end, an effective bicultural bridge will be built. A missionary's bonding to the local economy is first and foremost about his heart before his finances, standards of living, attire, and so on.[19]

One may say that a missionary should live in an affluent environment to fully recharge from challenging tasks he faces every day on the mission field. A missionary home on the mission field might as well need to provide a relaxed, comfortable setting after a day of hard work on the field. Many Western missionaries, therefore, have decided to create an affluent home environment that is similar to their homeside. They may have done so out of the pure reason of believing that it would eventually help them work more efficiently in the long run.

Again, the literature review rebuts such a possible opposing point. Only reasonable adjustments of the standard of living for the present

---

14. Kane, *Understanding Christian Missions*, 347–48.
15. See Muller et al., *Dictionary of Mission*; Anderson et al., *Mission Legacies*.
16. See Glover, *Bible Basis of Missions*.
17. Brewster and Brewster, *Bonding and the Missionary Task*, 465–69.
18. Ang, "Together-in-Difference."
19. See Anderson et al., *Mission Legacies*.

are suggested, which, by the way, can smoothly downgrade even further as time goes by and the missionary becomes more comfortable with the local life and, at the same time, the local economy eventually upgrades too. What matters the most is the missionary's willing heart to identify in every area with the locals he came to love. Friendship comes before work in a cross-cultural mission. Even so, friendship and relationship begin with the heart, and this is why the importance of the heart principle is addressed here. Without pertinent relationship-building based on mutual heart transmission, the work cannot be genuinely effective in the end.

If the nationals work with a missionary for the reason that he possesses more finances, education, and opportunities than them, it is unlikely to be a permanent, healthy channel for discipleship. A planted vision in their hearts that comes through the sharing of God's Word must be the ultimate ground for their cooperation.[20] They should work with a missionary not because of what he has but because of who he is. Also, friendship screens out true disciples from the false ones. Moreover, nationals are hungry for the sincere friendship of a missionary. V. S. Azariah, a well-known Indian bishop who served under British rule, once described the need for legitimate friendship in the life of missionaries.

> Through all the ages to come the Indian Church will rise up in gratitude to attest the heroism and self-denying labours of the missionary body. You have given your goods to feed the poor. You have given your bodies to be burned. We also ask for love. Give us friends![21]

Genuine cross-cultural discipleship takes place through genuine friendship transcending race and culture. Missionaries must be able to listen to the local people's opinions with an open mind. Ultimately, locals have been living there for thousands of years while the missionaries have relatively a shorter amount of time. Negligence to this warning may result in leading a Bohemian lifestyle of missionaries improperly tuned to the genuine needs of the community, a waste of precious resources given toward mission, and possibly temptation to make a false or insufficient report back home. One of the greatest assets of cross-cultural adaptation is the development of a listening heart. It stands out as crucial in all human relationships, including family life. It takes a missionary's servant-steward leadership to perk up a listening heart and kindle a considerate attitude toward the Master and others.

---

20. See LeFever, *Learning Styles*; Hendricks, *Teaching to Change Lives*.
21. Azariah, "Problem of Co-Operation between Foreign and Native Workers," 315.

There is good news though. As the local economy of the mission field grows over time, the national workers' income may also increase. Meanwhile, a missionary may learn to speak the local language fluently and get even more familiar with the ways to get around in local markets to buy things in a thriftier manner. The gap may likely be narrowed down as time passes by.

More homogenization also results in less friction when a missionary finds it necessary to discipline his local disciple. Being similar in kind narrows the relational gap, hence, confrontation becomes less alien but adds effectiveness. However, it needs to be noted that commitment is a subjective term rather than objective.[22] One cannot say to the other that he is not committed simply because the other does not do what one does. This fact applies even more so in the cross-cultural setting. It is a matter of the inward heart, which, of course, is portrayed by outwardly accompanying behaviors many times. However, commitment lies first in a person's attitude, not necessarily outcomes. The heart principle affirms that missionaries should try to experience bonding in their effort to adapt to the local lifestyle as a means to exercise an ministry style.

For a missionary to experience bonding in their effort to adapt to the local lifestyle as a means to exercise an ministry style, he should abide in the (1) kenosis (self-limitation) principle, (2) adjustment principle, and (3) heart principle. Every missionary aiming to have a successful disciple-producing ministry should make extra efforts toward the potential adaptation to the local lifestyle of the country where they're based.

For this reason, a call to action is raised for a missionary to consider a realistic minimum budget for his living on the mission field should he desire to see apparent fruits in cross-cultural discipleship. He should keep his heart open toward the needs and expectations of the national coworkers he works with. Developing trust and friendship should be his highest priority in missionary work.[23] Such an example is vividly shown in the earthly ministry of our Lord Jesus, the greatest cross-cultural disciple-maker that ever lived.

Lifestyle is, above all, a matter of one's heart and attitude. Even if it may be unrealistic for his family to live on a tenth of its living cost as soon as they arrive on the mission field, an incarnational missionary will keep on striving to be one of the locals, including in the area of standard of living. This will take time, and he and his family may never get to the economic level of their local coworkers but will keep cultivating the hearts and willingness to

---

22. Hull, *Jesus Christ, Disciplemaker*, 173.
23. See Sanders, *Spiritual leadership*; Cook, *Missionary Life and Work*.

pursue this noble agenda. Besides, a truthful, open mind and lifestyle will eventually earn the hearts of indigenous brothers who may come along his path of influence.[24] That should bring about a multitude of Christ's disciples made around him in due time.

A missionary's willingness to work toward cultural homogenization in their effort to adapt to the local economy and standard of living as a means to exercise the incarnational ministry style benefits his work. Let me conclude by saying that:

- Missionaries who are fond of the local food, clothing, and shelter tend to enjoy stronger bonding with indigenous coworkers.
- Missionaries who endeavor to pursue a modest living to fit into the local standard of living tend to experience stronger bonding with indigenous coworkers.
- Missionaries who voluntarily depend on local transportation means tend to discover stronger bonding with indigenous coworkers.
- Indigenous coworkers tend to find a stronger desire to befriend and model after missionaries who pursue cultural homogenization in their effort to adapt to the local economy and standard of living as a means to exercise the incarnational ministry style.

The pursuit of incarnational bonding with the local people whom missionaries and cross-cultural workers serve will ultimately result in the role-modeling of cross-cultural mentorship to penetrate on a deeper level.

HINDRANCES TO HOMOGENIZATION AND MULTIPLICATION

I'd like to point out four hindrances to overcome in order to experience biblical homogenization and discipleship multiplication in cross-cultural contexts. Each obstacle begins with the letter P.

1. Prematurity: This refers to reckless sending of missionaries in large quantities with only premature preparation. It is noteworthy that missionaries sent in the early church period were experienced and sharpened apostles and pastors. When it comes to missions, it is unfortunate that some Christians unfold their missionary work out of several unbiblical motivations. Three most deceptive motivations for missions I've observed are:

24. See Blackaby and Blackaby, *Spiritual Leadership*.

- Self-glorification (missions as adventure)
- Self-righteousness (missions as earning God's approval)
- Self-entertainment (missions as hedonism)

2. Pridefulness: This vulnerable human weakness imposes the superiority complex of the missionary and his sending body on mission fields. God's glory, *not* men's pride, is to be revealed in all the world through cross-cultural discipleship as people are purchased for God by the blood of Christ from every tribe, language, people, and nation (Revelation 5:9–14).

   There is a real need to escape from the neocolonial concept of mission. A substantial number of missionaries fail in the area of leaving permanent fruit of local disciples behind them who will carry on their legacy of life and work. It also wastes precious resources from their home front. Most of all, the neocolonial mission approach deteriorates missionaries' pure devotions to go and serve God's people at the Lord's command. They might end up returning home with some feelings of failure, which often leave a strong sense of mixed emotions of complaints toward people on the mission field and unresolved guilt toward themselves. Many times, such stories are not well reported back home.[25]

   When we consider that these missionaries are the one out of a hundred who have responded to the missionary call and made it to mission field, this phenomenon is implausibly alarming. It has risen as a huge obstacle to the church's missionary ventures, but very little has been said about it in the church world. It is because missionaries with such experiences usually do not share about their failures once they return home. They would rather wish to be treated as heroes back from spiritual battlefields. Therefore, it is not readily spoken out. Secondly, the success of a missionary's work should be measured rather by the local people who received benefits from the missionary, however, most of these locals do not have direct access to share with missionary's sending church and his supporters.[26]

   In this respect, even support for the locals (including financial support) must be made in a *paracletos* mode. It should not be just some sort of money-sending. It should portray the spirit of "companionship" in the world mission by literally going side by side with the indigenous church. Here is a biblical guideline to give financially

---

25. Yohannan, *Revolution in World Missions*, 155.
26. See Wakatama, *Independence for the Third World Church*, 51–65.

toward indigenous churches for proper cross-cultural discipleship to take root. Degrees of enculturation should be regarded here. Ugly bullying foreigners with some strings-attached agenda should be discouraged when giving takes place. Cross-cultural gospel workers should never behave this way. Both giver and receiver must remember that they are dealing with God's money, not their own! Stewardship with humility is indispensably required when financially supporting the local leaders. By the way, it is most often far better to give scholarships to indigenous leaders' education and training rather than just to give out support for immediate consumption. Investing in the future of people likely bears long-term fruits.

3. Paternalism: Paternalism is an unwillingness to let go of leadership to local leaders at the full bloom of missions work. This ill trait can be found in some mission organizations and missionaries, both Western and non-Western. Take the case of Korean missions. Although it was most influenced by John Nevius's Three Self strategy (self-support, self-propaganda, and self-governing), strangely and sadly enough, some Korean missions have practiced the least of the same principle on mission fields where they go and establish mission stations only to produce paternalistic local churches.[27] More will be discussed on the issue of paternalism in chapter 11.

4. Pastoral ministry orientation: This factor may be hard for some local church pastors to digest, but both goers and senders of missions should give the following questions a serious thought before launching a missionary enterprise. Is it a mission for the sake of the mission? Or is it a mission for the sake of the "empire" expansion of my pastoral ministry, church, or denomination? The mission is the very heartbeat of God. That is why the church exists. Nothing else can take its place and priority, even for the expectation of certain compensations in return. This is not biblical.

South Korea has grown in such a short period to be a missionary-sending nation from a missionary-receiving nation, cherishing the positive image of many American and European missionaries who came in the nineteenth century with attitudes to serve them, as opposed to many other countries of the same period receiving missionaries alongside colonial routes. The gospel has rarely witnessed significant breakthroughs in modern history in countries where it has entered either through or alongside colonization ventures. People's commitments to the message have been very

---

27. See Jang, "Is the Life of Korean missionaries exemplary?"

minimal. Discipleship has barely taken place in those countries because the colonial background fatally aggravated the genuine bonding efforts of both sides (missionary and indigenous people). It was once said that a pastor's resume is the people he has served when he leaves the church. Likewise, it may be also said that a missionary's resume must be the local people he has served when he leaves the mission field. Such long-lasting impact clings to the missionary's commitment toward cultural homogenization and incarnation with the locals during his tenure.

Another key principle to successful cross-cultural discipleship is the principle of *waiting*. Cultural homogenization also encourages indigenous ownership to take root. Cultural homogenization empowers the principle of waiting in cross-cultural discipleship. Discipleship is a continual stretching of the respective disciple's learning capacity per his potential. This keeps going on until he reaches the whole measure of the fullness of Christ. Should a discipler from an outside culture show his willingness to be in a bond with local disciples and their culture, they get encouraged to find dignity in their own cultural roots, thus indigenous ownership may be further enforced.

DISCUSSION AND REFLECTION QUESTIONS

1. To promote a missionary incarnate homogenization, the kenosis principle, adjustment principle, and heart principle were introduced in this chapter. Which of these resonated most with you as you read about them? What would be the most difficult principle for you to apply and why?

2. Lee coins the principle of "similar kind, less friction" to signify the incarnate homogenization of an effective cross-cultural gospel worker. How would you apply this principle in your cross-cultural discipleship? Please elaborate on it specifically.

3. In this chapter, four hindrances to homogenization and multiplication of missionary work were listed: prematurity, pridefulness, paternalism, and pastoral ministry orientation. Is there any area you're struggling with? Pray earnestly for God to examine your heart and mind about this.

11

Missionary Paternalism

This chapter explores both theological and missiological dimensions of the missionary paternalism epidemic in world mission. Missionary paternalism is a serious issue that has been hampering the missions effort of the body of Christ for centuries. It deters a sense of indigenous ownership of the very organization a missionary has founded on the mission field with years of the sweat of his brow. One of the most devastating symptoms of missionary paternalism is the fact that the missionary himself may not realize that he has a particular problem. Years of serving God on isolated foreign soil might have left him a distorted, self-satisfied person. He may be intoxicated with the fruits of the work of his hands and enjoy being the "man" of the organization because most of the locals who work with him are less educated and less experienced than him. As a result, the missionary's work may not proceed any further toward greater maturity and even succession to the coming generation of leadership. Eventually, it might as well hinder the fulfillment of the missionary's call.

ROOT PROBLEMS

Considerably, distrust is interpreted to be a root problem of missionary paternalism that underlies its concept. A missionary may say that he does not have trust yet in his national leaders and their capability to carry on the work he started years ago. Time and chance of succession to indigenous leadership can be postponed to a later period of his tenure on the mission field. Certainly, it takes years of preparation for someone of a heterogeneous cultural background to catch the missionary's vision, develop a suitable apprenticeship under his mentoring, and grow to full maturity. It is even likely that not everyone will make it through the process of discipleship, as we have seen it in Jesus' example. (Even the Son of God had a probability of eleven out of twelve!) Twists and turns are part of the disciple-making process. Nevertheless, Jesus' call to cross-cultural discipleship is uncompromisingly decreed in Matthew 28:19–20. Therefore, the temptation of missionary paternalism becomes an obstacle that every missionary who wishes to bear lasting fruits must overcome. The problem occurs when the missionary is not willing to take full responsibility of the disciple-making endeavor. To escape a notion of paternalism, however small local givings of funds, talent, and service may be in proportion to the entire demands of the mission, they must be appreciated and encouraged by a missionary. This vulnerability can be discovered even among veteran missionaries who have spent a lifetime on the mission field; no indigenous disciples would have been produced to take on their work in proper time. A number of the Western missionary-founded organizations face this peril on the mission field. When a missionary has to leave the field for reasons of health, furlough, and ministry call elsewhere, the organization faces closure and discontinuation of services it used to offer to the community. Good-willed enterprises will only end up leaving regrets for local people who once were beneficiaries of the missionary's ministry. Any property the organization possessed may fall into the hands of greedy individuals who wish to take advantage of the facility for personal gain. Often, such a case stirs up a lawsuit between home mission board and the locals, through which the Christian witness can be virtually impeded.

Missionary paternalism shows signs of excessive control by a missionary and inadequate training for future leadership. Ironically, should the missionary fail to prepare local disciples and be abruptly forced to leave the field, the premature release of authority may be considered and this can bring risk upon the organization. In most cases, unprepared national successors will not be able to discharge their duties, hence the work may collapse sooner or later. Besides, missionary paternalism has created negative responses over the years from national leaders of the Two-Thirds World mission fields. Lack of faithfulness and poor accountability among indigenous church leaders have recently grown more noticeable as a counterattack. They are not willing to take responsibility for something that is not theirs nor ever will be, so to speak. As a result, financial dishonesty and conning activities among national leaders have increased in the Two-Thirds World. Situations have been worsened when this factor has become an extra reason for missionaries to keep distrusting national leaders. The gap of mistrust continues to widen on both parties as a consequence.

The problem of distrust in missionary paternalism can be considered rather as a lack of trust in God, who called him to the mission field and, at the same time, who equally works in the hearts of the local people he serves with. The apostle Paul cheerfully commended the Gentile church leaders of Ephesus before his departure to Jerusalem in Acts 20:32: "And now I commend you to God, and to the word of his grace, which is able to build you up, and to give you the inheritance among all them that are sanctified." Paul demonstrated complete confidence that he who began a good work in his Philippian disciples would perfect it until the day of Jesus Christ (Philippians 1:6). He could trust his Gentile coworkers because he believed that Jesus himself would build his church and the gates of Hades would not prevail against it (Matthew 16:18). Because he trusted in God, the venerable apostle prepared leaders and successors during the tenure of his missionary service to the Gentiles.

A missiological probe on the issue of paternalism speaks similarly. The concept of paternalism is loosely linked with the colonialism that has swept the globe through two great wars of the modern age. The colonial era ended with World War II, however, the spirit of colonialism (or neocolonialism) still influences politics, society, and even the church world in degrees. The way people view Scripture is culturally screened and often deteriorated. Unfortunately, some Westerners fail to differentiate culture from Scripture. Such misunderstanding can cause deterioration of the gospel. It is colorfully portrayed among so-called prosperity gospel preachers' lucrative lifestyles and in their message of a God who is obliged to financially bless those who are spiritually sound. This teaching is neither applicable nor acceptable, say, in the Muslim world, where persecuted believers face the risks of hunger, arrest, and even possible death each day. It also entails that local leaders on the mission field who walk on their feet are not necessarily spiritually inferior to foreign missionaries who drive a four-wheel-drive jeep. William Wilberforce, an English politician who headed the anti-slavery campaign during Britain's colonial period, once described Christians who confuse Scripture with culture: "The result is that in the Christian world in the West, we settle for a cultural version of Christianity that is far from the real thing."[1]

THE ULTIMATE PERIL OF MISSION

The fates of missionary paternalism can be witnessed from Africa to Asia. Pius Wakatama, a Zimbabwean journalist, testifies:

1. Wilberforce, *Real Christianity*, 23–24.

> A certain mission built a well-equipped radio studio in Africa. The missionary director of the studio worked with a number of nationals in producing plays which were broadcast through the government operated national network. People responded positively to the programs. Many were finding Christ through them. The director of broadcasting of the government network wrote the studio a letter of commendation and encouragement. He mentioned that he appreciated the high moral tone of the programs. After a year the missionary, who alone could operate the recording console, had to come to America on furlough. Because there was no missionary to take over from him, the studio was closed and the work came to a stop. None of the Africans were trained to operate the console even though they could write scripts and dramatize the plays. Even today no nationals are being trained so as to continue that work. Instead that mission is now advertising in America for a missionary to go and direct the work of that studio. Is it surprising then that nationals are calling for a moratorium on missionaries? As long as more missionaries come they do not see any chance for themselves to be real leaders. They see their future as that of perpetual assistants.[2]

Another unfortunate case was reported from Asia. K. P. Yohannan, who heads the Gospel for Asia mission, shares his experience in his book *Revolution in World Missions*.

> I remember an incident—one of many—that illustrates this sad fact. During my days of preaching in the northwest of India I met a missionary from New Zealand who had been involved in Christian ministry in India for 25 years. During her final term she was assigned to a Christian bookstore. One day as my team and I went to her shop to buy some books, we found the book shop closed. When we went to her missionary quarters—which were in a walled mansion—we asked what was happening. She replied, "I am going back home for good." I asked what would happen to the ministry of the bookshop. She answered, "I have sold all the books at wholesale price, and I have closed down everything." With deep hurt, I asked her if she could have handed the store over to someone in order to continue the work. "No, I could not find anyone," she replied. I wondered why, after 25 years of being in India, she was leaving without one person whom she had won to Christ, no disciple to continue her work. She, along with her missionary colleagues, lived in

---

2. Wakatama, *Independence for the Third World Church*, 63.

walled compounds with three or four servants each to look after their lifestyle. She spent a lifetime and untold amounts of God's precious money, which could have been used to preach the gospel. I could not help but think Jesus had called us to become servants—not masters. Had she done so, she would have fulfilled the call of God upon her life and fulfilled the Great Commission. Unfortunately, this sad truth is being repeated all over the world of colonial-style foreign missions. Regrettably, seldom are traditional missionaries being held accountable for the current lack of results, nor is their failure being reported at home in the West.[3]

Overcoming missionary paternalism is not just a simple matter. It may involve more than a determination of the missionary himself on the field. The challenge may be tied with the home mission board that controls the mission fund and perhaps wishes to propagate their own denominationalism. An issue of stewardship must be raised at this point. Most donors who give financially to missions do so because they believe that their funds may contribute toward the expansion of God's kingdom. If the local disciples on the mission field mature and take over the work of the missionary, it should be considered as an advancement of the Great Commission. If untold millions are spent to keep the missionaries on the field while their work never becomes indigenized and in turn expands the kingdom of God, it is a critical matter of stewardship that needs to be tackled again as the church. Financial delinquency of church leaders has repeatedly increased to become a mockery of society in this day and age. The negative effect of missionary paternalism reaches far, even to the missionary's home country. Today, the church is being watched by society everywhere, especially in this area of financial stewardship.

In the end, neocolonialism-minded paternalism can seriously jeopardize a missionary's work according to the biblical definition of mission. It demeans the reproduction of Hesselgrave's Pauline cycle of mission.[4] When the gospel is preached to a group of audiences in any nation, David Hesselgrave asserts that they must grow mature to the point that they get to commission their own missionaries for other nations, thus the cycle repeats until all nations take part in world mission.

---

3. Yohannan, *Revolution in World Missions*, 164–65.
4. Hesselgrave, *Planting Churches Cross-Culturally*, 136.

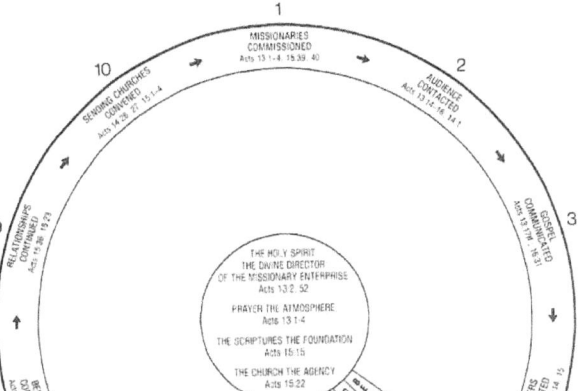

"... many of the Jews and of the God-fearing proselytes followed Paul and Barnabas..." (Acts 13:43).
"Not forsaking our own assembling together..." (Heb. 10:25).

(c) Hasselgrave 1980

V. S. Azariah described the devastating effect of missionary paternalism this way:

> The desire for independence and freedom of expression in political life was finding its counterpart in the religious world, and on this Azariah delivered his own balanced judgment: "Our young theologians want autonomy at one step; sober minds are willing to work more slowly but legitimate aspirations must be met." These he defined as follows: the curtailment of missionary power; the training of Indian leadership in the government of their own church; the preparation of the whole Christian community for indigenous leadership and self-support.[5]

---

5. Anderson et al., *Mission Legacies*, 326.

The mission is a task given by the Lord Jesus himself to his *universal* church, and this requires participation and stewardship from international communities. Missionary paternalism severely tampers this God-given agenda for the church today.

DISCUSSION AND REFLECTION QUESTIONS

1. Lee writes that distrust is interpreted to be a root problem of missionary paternalism and that it can also be considered as a lack of trust in God, who calls both missionaries and local leaders for his kingdom task. Do you agree or disagree?

2. In line with the Pauline cycle of David Hesselgrave, the Great Commission should be recycled and multiplied. World mission isn't a proprietorship of certain nations or groups any longer. All born-again believers in all nations (*ethne*) must be somehow conducive to the multiplication of the Great Commission. How would you respond to this global challenge, and what can you do to be a part of it?

3. It is the responsibility of both a goer and a sender to overcome the temptation of paternalism together to build a healthy church and advance God's kingdom among the nations. How would you encourage a missionary to overcome paternalism, and what can you do to help make this happen?

12

The Church Construction Model on the Mission Field

BUILDING GOD'S HOUSE?

During my tenure as a career missionary serving extensively different communities of Africa and Asia, it was observed that concerns might arise on the issue of church construction when the time is reached that local churches have increased in their membership and to have faced the need of their own facilities for worship. If the congregation has had either a missionary foundation or any form of missionary connection, this need sometimes develops into frictions between the local church and foreign mission, and the majority of disputes surround the source of funding and style of construction.

Many foreign mission boards have held onto their policy of church building style. If all or the majority of funding for church construction derived from a missionary or a mission, the fund often comes with certain expectations and conditions. Denominational foreign missions particularly wish for the churches under their umbrella to demonstrate uniformity in their building styles, and frequently the Western church building style is imposed in this case. On the other hand, most local churches prefer to have their own idea and design for the building style—often the local style that suits their community environment and culture. National leaders will hardly refuse the foreign assistance of funding for their construction, whether the church is capable of raising the entire construction funds on their own or the church's fundraising capacity is just inadequate to raise the funds on their own. Nevertheless, most national leaders want to take the initiative in deciding on construction details. To this end, this research was made to critically examine root issues of the widespread phenomena in missions today and afterward to suggest a way forward for an ideal church construction model on the mission field.

A local church is a manifest expression of the kingdom of God in the society where it is situated, both at home and on the mission field. It is linked with its head—Christ, who is seated at the right hand of God (Mark 16:19)—that reaches down to the particular community as a reflection of heaven. A local church, at the leading of the Holy Spirit, who communicates through church leadership (as in the case of Acts 13:1–2), should be able to exercise freedom of autonomy in church affairs in conjunction with other fraternal congregations near and far. This freedom certainly extends to even the details of church construction. A local church knows the culture, legal relations, needs, and flavor of her local community. Her members are from that community, so they know what type of church building may facilitate effective community evangelism and not hinder it.

LOCAL STYLE OR WESTERN STYLE

Any vivid strength of the Western-style building structure can be, and should be, learned for and adapted to church construction on the mission field. The root problem, however, lies with the issue of control. Desire to control the affairs of local churches on the mission field often traces its roots to the concept of neocolonialism.[1] The foreign mission and missionaries may consider and treat national church leaders as those who cannot manage their own church matters and therefore need outside "intervention" from the paternalistic perspective, along with some financial contribution.

---

1. Muller et al., *Dictionary of Mission*, 69.

Picture 8. Church construction in Malawi

Michael Youssef, a former managing director of the Haggai Institute, makes a point on the issue of mistakes some Western missionaries make in this regard.

> Many well-intentioned missionaries in the nineteenth and twentieth centuries went to Africa and Asia seeking to evangelize those cultures for Christ. Unfortunately, some of them could not separate the Christian gospel from their Western culture. When they planted churches in those countries, the missionaries often imported Western art, music, and architecture. They built churches that would have been better suited for Boston or London than for a village in the Third World. They told these new Christians that their indigenous forms of music were heathen, and that they needed to sing the sacred music of Isaac Watts and Charles Wesley—music that was completely alien and incomprehensible to them.[2]

Insisting on Western styles in non-Western countries may only evoke either indifference or repulsion of local church members toward the

---

2. Youssef, *Leadership Style of Jesus*, 51.

construction project.³ Perhaps there is a need for Western missionaries and Western mission boards to carefully and honestly reexamine their hearts on this matter.

Glover warns of the superiorism of Western Christianity in his gentle yet profound message that was addressed in his book *The Bible Basis of Missions*.

> As to the Westerner's smug feeling of superiority, it would be well for him to dip back into the earlier centuries and note the condition of his "Occidental" forbears in Europe before the gospel was first brought to that continent by "Oriental" missionaries from Asia, and to remember that Christianity originated in that continent, not in Europe, much less in America. No, any superiority we may boast over the peoples of the East is not inherent in us, but is to be attributed to the uplifting influences and the great advantages of every kind which the gospel has brought to us.⁴

Romans 1:14 reminds anyone involved in the missions enterprise that, "I am debtor both to Greeks and to Barbarians, both to the wise and to the foolish." Surprisingly, for Paul being indebted was the preliminary biblical qualification of sharing the gospel with the heathens. Jesus' idea of a foreign mission for his body was the compulsive act overwhelmed by his Calvary love (2 Corinthians 5:14). It is based on humility, not on a lording attitude. Jesus' exemplary teaching on the humility of the missionary attitude has attained the highest perfection through self-limitation. Perhaps it is now time for Western Christians to be reminded of Jesus' missionary philosophy, which was based on humility, perfectly expressed in his incarnational approach. The incarnation of a missions organization, missionary, strategy, church construction, and even funding may need to be reconsidered in this regard.⁵

INDIGENOUS FUNDING OR FOREIGN FUNDING

An ideal church construction model on the mission field, whether a church is built in the local style with indigenous funding or in the Western style with foreign funding, requires the local church's autonomous and contextualized effort to reach out to the given community. Should a foreign mission get involved with the financing, concept, and manpower for the building

3. Muller et al., *Dictionary of Mission*, 69.
4. Glover, *Bible Basis of Missions*, 190.
5. Langmead, *Word Made Flesh*, 217.

project, it is suggested that this be done within the parameters of the incarnational approach, which is control-free and has no strings attached. All in all, church construction should be done for better evangelism and outreach for the community, which will end up glorifying God. If this initial purpose is put aside, church construction may invite meaningless struggles over control and eventual waste of resources.

The message of the gospel can be contextualized into any culture without friction, if presented correctly. It is the only religious propaganda that is transmitted, without the language or originating culture of its founder.[6] It is this gospel, when preached to individuals, that gives birth to a church with produced converts. It is for the propagation of the same gospel that a local church should consider the construction of facilities. Therefore, church construction, whether it is done in the local style or the Western style, whether it is done with indigenous funding or foreign funding, is a matter of convenience, not of absolutes.

KEY PRINCIPLES TO CONSIDER

However, four principles need to be addressed when it comes to church construction on the mission field. Again, they are the four P factors, namely: (1) price, (2) provision, (3) proof, and (4) priority. First, the price of the land and building materials should be considered. Secondly, local provisions must be thought out before construction. Generally, price and provision are two closely related matters. Most locally produced building materials are cost-effective and have an ample supply with minimal transport charges. For instance, in the Ngong community of suburban Nairobi, Kenya, quarries are locally present and stones can be economically employed as church building materials. In eastern Uganda and Lilongwe, Malawi, local soils are quite suitable for burning bricks. Bricks can be purchased or even be locally made in those regions without much financial stress. In some areas of the world, cement is locally produced; hence using more cement than other building materials may save expense. Following the rationality of local provision can greatly utilize the funds and valuable resources gathered. Thirdly, a principle of proof needs to be considered. Roofing a church with metallic materials such as iron sheets may not be a good idea in coastal regions of Kenya, where the heat elevates during the dry seasons. Local weatherproof materials must be used to provide an appropriate environment for worshippers. Most times, the locals are familiar with such information and may have faster and cheaper access to those materials than

---

6. Sanneh, *Whose Religion Is Christianity?*, 98.

foreigners. Last but not least, the priority of a sense of ownership must be in high regard for church construction to be wisely administered on the mission field. The local church and her members should have affection and commitment toward the construction effort in one way or another. If not, foreign funds may pour in from abroad to construct a beautiful sanctuary, but no one will remain responsible to maintain the facility later. Local church members with a sense of ownership will invest their finance, land, labor, time, and prayer toward the construction of their own worship center, however small it may be in proportion of giving. After all, Jesus was honored and the miracle of provision took place upon the small giving of a little lad.[7] By and far, the sense of ownership must be prioritized for the effective construction and maintenance of a church on the mission field.

Even the motivation of foreign funding for church construction on the mission field must be reexamined at this point. The secular idea that a donor with more contribution controls the organization is not only unhealthy but also unbiblical. As mentioned earlier in this chapter, a local church should be led by the Holy Spirit, who communicates through church leadership. It was in this context that Philip Potter preferred the term "companionship" over "partnership" to describe foreign funding and the relationship between donor and organization for the cause of mission. He did so because the term "partner," which implied, in the original sense of the word, a division of property, no longer sufficed; instead of this, one should rather talk of "companionship," that is, those who eat bread together.[8] The common good of the Great Commission is the goal every nation must run together toward. One may do so with money while others may do so with manpower, and others with prayers, and others with ideas, and the list goes on. The word "companionship" even sounds more cooperative, while "partnership" implies divisiveness. Companions, or coworkers, therefore should respect mutual equality and the roles of various parts of the universal body of Christ to reach the common vision through their cooperation.

On this pretext, foreign funding is suggested to serve only as a booster on top of the indigenous effort to build their own church. It has been our discovery on mission fields in Africa and Asia that people rarely show lasting commitments in projects they do not take part in any way. Daniel Weightman observed during his missionary tenure in the Bahamas that the self-funding effort of the indigenous ministry team is vital for the success of projects on the mission field.

---

7. Glover, *Bible Basis of Missions*, 202–3.
8. Muller et al., *Dictionary of Mission*, 340.

In order for a sizable donor base to be established and maintained, fundraising strategies need to be nurtured. Missionaries need to play their role too, providing training and expertise, as well as being an example of modest living. Multifaceted fundraising initiatives need to happen on both the national level, through the efforts of an indigenous Board of Directors and locally through volunteer leaders. As a result, ministry will eventually move toward being self-funded and there will be adequate resources available to meet the demands of ministry; staff can be hired, appropriate transportation can be purchased and camping equipment can be acquired.[9]

When it comes to the matter of local style with indigenous funding versus the Western style with foreign funding for church construction, an idea of the blend of both may be also suggested as long as a sense of national ownership is not demoted in the project. Foreign donation for a matching-fund program to assist national church construction can excel in leaving a long-lasting impact, provided proper administration and accountability in the procedure. A short-term missionary team of youths may be sent to a mission field to serve as volunteer church-builders in cooperation with national believers and under the supervision of indigenous leaders. At EAPTC, we've seen such methodologies work ideally as the mission organization has tried to bridge foreign donors and volunteers with local churches in Africa and Asia for mutual companionship toward mission advancement.

The subject of adaptation must be carefully implemented when one is dealing with cross-culture missionary work. True faith is always about relationship with Christ, not about rules and regulations. Others are secondary subjects. Woodbridge speaks of the apostle Paul, who set a significant milestone on this issue.

> Paul has left abundant legacies behind. Some of his legacies may be easily forgotten, therefore, they need to be mentioned here. . . . True faith is not about rules and regulations. God does not deal with people like an accountant. God enables his people to share His love with others by imparting the Spirit of Christ in their hearts when they accept His grace.[10]

Paul's dealing with the Gentile circumcision issue has been left to us as a missions legacy today. Perhaps the same principle can be applied today to our missions endeavors as we strive to follow the footsteps of the venerable

---

9. Weightman, "Essential Components," 81.
10. Woodbridge, *Great Leaders of the Christian Church*, 38.

missionary. The same principle can be expected to apply to church construction styles on mission fields.

As long as the church building manifests God's grace and provides shelter for God's people to worship more freely and to propagate the contextualized message of the gospel further in the community, it does not matter whether a church is built in the local style and with domestic funding, or in the Western style and with foreign funding, or by a blend of both. What matters the most will be the effective establishment of a local church, the body of Christ, that grows toward self-propagation, self-government, and self-support, as Henry Venn advocated.[11] Construction efforts of indigenized churches that self-propagate, self-govern, and self-support[12] can be assisted by finances or by other means without creating dependency on foreign help. The key issue of church construction on the mission field is the indigenization that may bring about ownership and stewardship of national churches, not local style and indigenous funding versus Western style and foreign funding. In the end, it is the kingdom of our God that advances when local churches settle and grow on the mission field.

DISCUSSION AND REFLECTION QUESTIONS

1. Do you believe that a local church is a manifest expression of the kingdom of God in the society where it is situated? If yes, how would you see this statement applied in terms of church construction style on the mission field?

2. In this chapter, four principles were addressed to consider while constructing a church facility on the mission field. To facilitate a church construction that promotes indigenous ownership and flourishes the kingdom of God in the nations, begin by honestly considering the following four P factors:

- Price (financial planning)
- Provision (accessibility of building materials)
- Proof (environment-friendly)
- Priority (sense of ownership)

    Which areas do you or your mission find weakness among these four P factors? What can you do to strengthen the weaknesses?

11. Anderson et al., *Mission Legacies*, 137.
12. Anderson et al., *Mission Legacies*, 194.

3. Lee reminds us, "A subject of adaptation must be carefully implemented when one is dealing with cross-cultural missionary work. True faith is always about relationship with Christ, not about rules and regulations." How have you seen this mistake made on the mission field?

13

The Final Frontier

THE ENDS OF THE EARTH?

Please let me wrap up my discussion with this legitimate and inevitable question. Is there a "final frontier" for missions? Or is missions supposed to be a final frontier in itself? Where is the "ends of the earth" that Jesus referred to in Acts 1:8 at the very last hour of his incarnate life on earth after the resurrection? Wouldn't this be of some priority and significance if Christ said it just before he left?

I have met missionaries who bluntly claim their mission field to be the final frontier of missions. The list varies from North Korea to Israel, and many more. While I certainly value and appreciate the uniqueness and specialness of their call to a specific place God has called them to serve, I'd like to encourage us to first consider what the Lord Jesus indicated concerning the parameters of our missions mandate:

> ... You will be my witnesses in Jerusalem, and in all Judea and Samaria, and to the ends of the earth. (Acts 1:8b)

Those places—Jerusalem, Judea, Samaria, and the ends of the earth—are known as the M-categories in missiological terms. However, it was Jesus, the Commander-in-Chief of the Great Commission, who created the earth and knew it to be round. To put it in other words, it is sensible to say that one's own Jerusalem somehow equates to his own end of the earth. Thus, Jesus' parameter of "Jerusalem . . . and to the ends of the earth" was not meant to be sequential but rather categorical about one's missional influence.

Vocabularies like "missions," "world mission," and "missionary" do not appear in the Bible. Nonetheless, the underlying concept of the entire Bible aims at missions. There were no professional missionaries who were specialized in overseas missionary work in the early church. Some Jewish diasporas (probably the Hebraic Jews) preached to fellow Jews while others (probably the Hellenistic Jews) did so to Gentiles (Acts 11:20). There was only a fine line between monocultural workers and cross-cultural workers. Geography and ethnicity didn't seem to matter much to the missions endeavors of the early church believers. Probably, there wasn't much need for it because the vicinity of the Middle East and surrounding nations were compatible under Roman political influence and Greek cultural influence. Every Christian was "on the move" to share the Way wherever they were scattered to and whomever they met on their paths.

Statistically, the latest world missions trend shows that missionaries are being sent out from everywhere to everywhere through everywhere. Strategists have previously noticed that Africa, along with Asia, would emerge as the key fulcrum for world missions in the twenty-first century. The 2010 Lausanne Congress held in South Africa validated that to be true.[1]

At the dusk of reaching the rest of the unreached people groups (UPGs) that remained, with only several thousand, the body of Christ was rejoicing at the possibility of seeing the soon return of our Lord, assuming that the Great Commission was about to be fulfilled. As it so happened that the wave of secularization in Europe, the continent that had enjoyed blossoming Christian culture for centuries, devastated the ecclesial impact on society and brought about the unavoidable need of re-evangelizing the region. This phenomenon left missiologists puzzled at what might be the next step. It was at this timely turn of the missiological perspective that churches began to contemplate deeper on the concept of the *missio Dei*. They sought out the heart of God at this juncture and came to perceive that the Bible pertaining to the fulfillment of the Great Commission points rather to the manifestation of the *missio Dei*. Therefore, Christian leaders from around the world saw the need for prioritizing the kingdom of God manifested in every aspect of believers' lives as the contemporary agenda. From my religious neighbor living the next door to a hidden tribe in the deepest jungle of Amazon, the kingdom lifestyle is to be promoted and emphasized. This tells us that whether you're a preacher, politician, businessman, housewife, or truck driver, you have a part to play in this grand *missio Dei*. We need to reach out

---

1. Dowsett, *Cape Town Commitment*, 2.

and model a lifestyle of multiplying disciples both at home (beginning with my own family) and in the remaining UPGs at a distance.

GOD'S KINGDOM COME

It must be the prayer of every born-again believer that God's kingdom come on earth, near and far (Matthew 6:10; Luke 11:2). We live in a "glocal" era—rightfully so, as we consider unprecedented God-given tools given into our hands, from transportation methods to communication tools. The world has become smaller and more within our reach than ever before. It is imperative that we live as messengers of Christ in our own worlds, both in monocultural and cross-cultural contexts. Whether we serve as a sender or a goer at this present moment, we're to practice a witnessing lifestyle whatever we do, wherever we go, and whomever we meet. Such missional influences may stay in one's locality or extend to a foreign country. A sender is as important as a goer in the *missio Dei* because our call is first and foremost about the Caller before it is about the place. As Christian, it is our Heavenly Father's will to embrace the places, times, and peoples God has put on our paths as our mission fields (Acts 17:26).

Sometimes I feel that EAPTC is likened to this hundred-year-old tree that I captured on camera on the campus of Ebenezer Bible College and Seminary in Zamboanga, Philippines, during a week of my teaching there. What began a quarter-century ago as a vision of one Korean American missionary couple serving in Kenya has now grown into hundreds of churches, training centers, schools, orphanages, and microfinance ministries reaching out to communities and nations. The outstretching influence of thousands of EAPTC training programs' alumni have built a fort of havens where individuals get to find the salvation of their souls and kingdom life of their journey in Jesus. Scores of short-term missionaries who have visited us and worked with us on the EAPTC fields attest to that. On top of that, the global impact is felt through the books and articles written by veteran EAPTC leaders, alongside the ongoing training sessions that are taught by them both in classrooms and online around the world.

The tree may not look so clean or straight at a glance, but it certainly has a natural, alive, and promising energy vibrantly flowing from the root to trunk, branches, and leaves. This tree is slowly but steadily growing, both inside and outside. Deeply rooted in the same spiritual DNA, vision, and mission, greater maturity has developed over the years. Thanks to each part of the body with various gifting and functions, it has expanded to an international scope with its presence in the nations of Africa and Asia. I pray every day that the Lord will continue to nurture this dream tree to reach out deeper and further in our richness of diversity and unity, as many more nationalities, ethnicities, and generations are added and represented in the body of EAPTC.

I'm convinced that God is still willing and able to use *anyone* who is committed to following him and his missions mandate to "go and make disciples of all nations." Romans 2:11 affirms that "there is no favoritism of persons with God" (KJV). One of the most important people to make disciples of is our own family members, particularly the children God has given to us. Discipleship is a starting point of world missions, and it should begin with my own house. Ripples of the disciple-making lifestyle at home become the waves that impact our ministries. Biblical discipleship is a way of life before it is a church program. After all, world missions begin from home missions. Family is a building block of every great Christian social movement in history. Cross-cultural discipleship is based on family, one huge family of various cultures and subcultures. At the same time, it begins with the smallest unit of one family that agrees, prays for, and supports together a missionary working for the greater family. Almost one out of every three missionaries may become a victim of family breakdown.[2] Hence, the family relationship is of great importance in missionary life in the field. Involving his family members to serve together in the work of missions should help. The impact of discipleship at home can, and will, disseminate to our own Judea, Samaria, and the nations. Some mighty preachers and missionaries

---

2. Van Meter, "US Report of Findings on Missionary Retention."

missed out on raising their children to be disciples. We're called to go and make disciples of our own children as much as we're called to the nations.

Besides, look around you and ask God to show you the person he wants you to influence for godly discipleship. If you don't see one, ask the Lord of the harvest to send you someone on your path. Invest your God-given time, talent, and resources to help the person to mature as a committed follower of Christ. That's the ultimate and biblical methodology for you to eventually mature yourself as Christ's disciple. Rather strange yet profound, the Bible doesn't have any command for us to *be* a disciple. It only says, over and over, *make* disciples.

Luke 9:23 and 14:27 challenge us to take up our cross daily and follow Christ in order to be his disciple. Parental love is precious and is cherished and appreciated in almost every culture. Certainly, most parents give birth to their children and raise them at the cost of pain and sacrifice. Most of us begin to understand and to truly appreciate the great love of our own parents when we become parents ourselves. It is the same with our spiritual life. We begin to understand the love of God in greater depth when we minister to others and try to follow God's call in our lives. The Bible calls this effort "carrying our cross." When our heart may be pierced with nails of disappointment, discouragement, and even false accusation, while we're trying to win and raise others for Christ, many of us may begin to better comprehend the meaning of God's love toward us in depth. When we make disciples of others, both near and far, only then do we get to find the blessing of becoming a bona fide disciple of Christ.

Sometimes, I envision that rapturous moment when I will get to enter into the other side of eternity and finally meet my Lord Jesus face to face. In an ecstasy of joy over his loving welcome and glorious presence, I'm sure I'll be lost in time. I take pleasure in imagining people of different nations, cultures, and skin colors coming to greet me afterward. The depiction of greeting and being greeted by multitudes of people from various tribes and languages and nations that ended up in heaven through the blessing and influence of my missional life on earth brightens my days—even more so when I'm downcast.

Nations still desire God's messengers to be sent to them to share his truth. Romans 10:11–13 confirms it by saying:

> Anyone who believes in him will never be put to shame. For there is no difference between Jew and Gentile—the same Lord is Lord of all and richly blesses all who call on him, for everyone who calls on the name of the Lord will be saved.

Nina Gunter once said, "If you take missions out of the Bible, you won't have anything left but the covers."[3] Where you are today is rightfully the final frontier of missions. Can you sense the eyes of the Lord ranging throughout the earth to strengthen those whose hearts are fully committed to him and his Great Commission (2 Chronicles 16:9)?

Allow me to leave you with these questions. What can you offer to God to make disciples out of the people within your influence, near and far? How would you bless the world out of what God has blessed you with? Where would you let God's kingdom come in the parameters of your life?

DISCUSSION AND REFLECTION QUESTIONS

1. Lee states that, considering the earth being round, it is sensible to say that one's own Jerusalem equates to his own end of the earth. Do you agree or disagree? If you do, where do you believe is your own "end of the earth" that Jesus wants to reach through you?

2. Look around you today and ask God to show you the person He wants you to influence for godly discipleship. If you don't see one, ask the Lord of the harvest to send you someone on your path. When God leads you to the person, invest your God-given time, talent and resources to help him to mature as a committed follower of Christ.

3. Take some time to envision what God has in store for you to redeem this world for Christ. What can you specifically offer to God to make disciples out of the people within your influence, near and far?

---

3. Tilley, *Mission America*, 41.

Epilogue

Psalm 37 consecutively indicates God's willingness to give his people the land for an inheritance:

> Verse 9: ... Those who hope in the Lord will *inherit the land*.
> Verse 11: ... The meek will *inherit the land* ...
> Verse 22: Those the Lord blesses will *inherit the land* ...
> Verse 29: The righteous will *inherit the land* ...
> Verse 34: ... He will exalt you to *inherit the land* ...

This is precisely my prayer for you as you continue to pursue a missional life God has called you to live out. This world belongs to our Lord, and all authority in heaven and on earth has been given to him (Matthew 28:18). In Jesus, we can claim the lands of the nations for Christ even as Caleb claimed Hebron to be his inheritance by faith and perseverance before it was to be conquered (Joshua 14:12). The nations yearn for God's message to be heard through his messengers.

> ... How shall they hear without a preacher? And how shall they preach, except they be sent? ... (Romans 10:14–15, KJV)

This biblical mandate articulates what Eunice and I have been doing for the world mission for decades. From the dusty land of Malawi in Central Africa to a missionary-barred China, church leadership trainings are currently ongoing around the world. As a result, new churches are constantly planted and existing churches strengthened in countless communities. Empowered local churches are sequentially encouraged to engage in societal transformation through school ministry, microfinance projects, agricultural ministry, orphanages, and so forth. Many of our churches within the EAPTC network shine Christ's light by bringing godly and positive changes in the locality. In the face of the challenges of war, famine, poverty, and disease, our workers seek to be the salt that Jesus expects us to be. This is what we at EAPTC believe God has called us to do. Even at IGSL, where Eunice and

I cooperate with Cru to raise leaders for Asian churches, we're committed to equipping *servant-steward leaders* for over twenty Asian countries. It is through their skillful works that Eunice and I expect to see God's kingdom come in the regions where his light is still dim.

Effective cross-cultural gospel ministry advances around three characteristics, as I've discussed in this book. Jesus, the greatest Missionary of all time, must have known the best way to reach the world unto himself. He has focused his missionary journey on earth on the following three distinctive areas.

First, the Son of God became one with the locals in Palestine. Nearly 90 percent (thirty of thirty-three years) of his earthly life was spent on incarnate homogenization with Jews. He wasn't ashamed to be identified with the mankind he came to love and save. This is a perfect model of incarnate homogenization out of love.

Secondly, Jesus concentrated on small-group discipleship during the remaining 10 percent of the days of his flesh. Margaret Mead once said that "a small group of thoughtful people could change the world. Indeed, it's the only thing that ever has."[1] It only takes a handful of absolutely determined and united people to change the world because the biblical principle of multiplication is still applicable. We can see from the strategies of twelve tribes, twelve disciples, and even the tithing principle that not a small percentage of great works of our missionary God has been birthed out of the multiplicative nature of tiny seeds. One person disciples a small group of other disciples, and each discipled disciple becomes a discipler to disciple others again. The cycle repeats to multiply more groups of other disciples, and the influence keeps on expanding to the nations. A fraction of giving as a token of our submission to the Lord also gets reproduced to bear fruits of the gospel.

While some animals are capable of mass reproduction, no human babies can be born that way. Even twins and triplets are rare in natural human birth. It is one of the major differences between the creation of nature and mankind. In the beginning, God created nature en masse, but when it came to the human beings he created only two. It conveys the message that humans, engraved with the *imago Dei*, have a distinctive value that can be found in no other creature. The same principle applies in the spiritual dimension. It isn't feasible or biblical to produce genuine disciples of Christ en masse. The Son of God knew this and chose a small-group discipleship strategy to win the world for the Father. It is sometimes unfathomable to grasp the idea that the Creator of the gigantic universe is mindful of mankind

---

1. Lutkehaus, *Margaret Mead*, 261.

and that he cares for dust-like human beings by showing them his personal interest and giving his undivided attention (Psalm 8:4). Likewise, bona fide disciples can be produced only by individual care and personalized mentoring. This is one significant angle that seminary education shouldn't be blind to and miss out on. Mature leaders aren't manufactured by mass factory-like training. Today, many Christian leaders need more than theological education. They're hungry for mentors whom they can look up to and model themselves after, either nearby or from afar. That is the only way theological training does not end up producing "copycat" leaders but seasoned leaders in the body of Christ. Personal care and considerate touches are essential in discipleship, both in monocultural and cross-cultural contexts.

Christianity started from one person—Jesus—and has multiplied through his church. Most evangelicals agree that the foundation of the church is linked to the apostle Peter by virtue of his confession of Christ (Matthew 16:15–18). Inspired by the Holy Spirit, Peter was able to confess that Jesus is the Christ and the Son of the living God after a series of character-shaping discipleship moments he previously encountered with Jesus. Christian discipleship should be founded upon one's character-building transformation, not merely on the visible results shown in one's missionary work, evangelistic effort, and pastoral ministry. One's *being* should be examined more than *doing*. The administrative system for ministry expansion certainly has its merits, but people-building holds a higher priority. If we focus on building people, people will build the ministry. Systems, programs, curricula, and facilities are simply tools to build the people of God. Another biblical model for the multiplication of cross-cultural discipleship is discovered in Paul's ministry in Ephesus (Acts 19:1–10). As clearly demonstrated by the apostle Paul, both fatherly heart and administrative skills should be manifested in a balanced way for effective discipleship.

EAPTC has faithfully kept two objectives as focal points of its ministry among the many branched forms of its missionary enterprise. They are (1) to empower local churches to be small-group training centers to recruit and train leaders, and (2) to facilitate them to plant new churches with the help of mother churches, preferably looking to unreached peoples and the nations. Those small groups have kept multiplying, in the form of either discipleship-based Bible training centers or daughter churches across the communities and nations of Africa and Asia. The kingdom of God is expanding through the disciples raised in the nations and for the nations. Even the students and graduates of IGSL, who were personally mentored by an international team of faculty members during their two to three years of on-campus study, continue to cause transformation all over Asia. Personal mentorship in a small-group setting is strategic in leadership formation.

Lastly, the Lord Jesus demonstrated a sacrificial life for his people through the cross. The Son of God was willing to give his everything for the locals and even to die for them. This love compels today's cross-cultural workers to voluntarily lay down their rights and privileges and serve people of not their own on the mission field, following Christ's example. A missional person is someone who becomes overwhelmed by the extravagant love of Christ and responds to his call.

God's heart is after all nations. It runs after them. It beats for their salvation. You and I just need to keenly sense what the Holy Spirit wants to do and is doing in this generation and participate right in the center of it. Hence, everything—I mean everything—takes God's grace in the work of mission. We must always remember, Jesus is indeed the Commander-in-Chief of the world mission.

Having followed Christ to America, Africa, and Asia, Eunice and I have learned that life is not about where to live but rather how to live and whom to live for. It is not about just getting my blessings but sharing my blessings with the world around me. From the biblical perspective, everyone who breathes on earth has a purpose to fulfill. To live that out, one must align his heart, worldview, and life-view to those of the Designer. Some Christians think that missions is for overseas and evangelism for the locality. Some even perceive that missions is just a church program. In fact, mission is the underlying theme of the entire redemptive history overlaid by God from Genesis to Revelation. Meanwhile, evangelism is the tool with which the body of Christ was called to complete the mission. If the frame of a car represents the mission, its engine is evangelism. Similarly, the mission can be compared to a human body and evangelism to the heart.

A missional Christian exists for the mission. He lives with purpose and resists a self-centered life. The person carries his cross and follows Christ daily. I believe in the call of each born-again believer on earth. For Christ, the cross was his life purpose. It was the reason for which he was born and lived. Our Lord Jesus was never distracted from running toward his calling. He did not meet everybody on earth to preach, teach, and heal. There is no biblical record to support that he traveled outside of the small vicinity of Palestine in his public ministry days. In other words, he did not do everything during his incarnational ministry. His earthly ministry was concentrated but full of impact. Every one of Christ's disciples, including you and me, has a unique call to fulfill before our last breath on earth. Living for this missional call and dying for it will make our life count toward carrying our own cross.

The essence of the Great Commission is about making disciples of different nations by entering into their world by crossing cultures. The task of the Great Commission is set to develop around the ministry of cross-cultural discipleship. Every Christian is called to the mission in one way or another, as a goer, sender, promoter, encourager, giver, and so on. When each one does his part, it'll eventually fill the earth with God's glory to fulfill the prophecy of Habakkuk:

> For the earth will be filled with the knowledge of the glory of the
> Lord as the waters cover the sea. (Habakkuk 2:14)

What is *your* call toward God's mission? Are you ready and available for God to use you, either as a goer or sender or maybe as both and more, for what he is doing in this generation for his grand vision of the *missio Dei*? Are you willing to let God make your life counted worthy in this world and eternity? I pray you are.

ARE YOU . . .
Called from the nations?
Called into the nations?
Called for the nations?

Christ is mobilizing an army
of his disciples from the nations.
His commission to go and make disciples
still remains the same.

To fulfill this Great Commission,
we need more workers to raise disciples
from all walks of life and sectors of society.

**Learn more about the works of
EAPTC International.**

goeaptc.com

Bibliography

Adeney, Miriam. *Kingdom Without Borders: The Untold Story of Global Christianity.* Downers Grove, IL: InterVarsity, 2009.

Ainsworth, Mary S., and John Bowlby. "An Ethological Approach to Personality Development." *American Psychologist* 46.4 (1991) 333–41.

Amadeo, Kimberly. "What Is Considered Middle-Class Income?" *The Balance*, April 9, 2020. https://www.thebalance.com/definition-of-middle-class-income-4126870.

Anderson, Gerald H., Robert T. Coote, Norman A. Horner, and James M. Philips. *Mission Legacies: Biographical Studies of Leaders of the Modern Missionary Movement.* Maryknoll, NY: Orbis, 1994.

Ang, Ien. "Together-in-Difference: Beyond Diaspora, into Hybridity." *Asian Studies Review* 27.2 (2003) 141–154.

Azariah, V. S. "Problem of Co-Operation between Foreign and Native Workers. III." In *The History and Records of the Conference*, World Missionary Conference, vol. 9, 306–15. New York: Revell, 1910. http://ia600406.us.archive.org/6/items/reportofcommissio9worl/reportofcommissio9worl.pdf.

Barna Group. "Silent and Solo: How Americans Pray." Research Releases in Faith & Christianity, August 15, 2017. https://www.barna.com/research/silent-solo-americans-pray.

Bell, Steve. *Gospel for Muslims: Learning to Read the Bible through Eastern Eyes.* Milton Keynes, UK: Authentic Media, 2012.

Blackaby, Richard, and Henry Blackaby. *Spiritual Leadership.* Nashville: B&H, 2011.

Borthwick, Paul. *Western Christians in Global Mission: What's the Role of the North American Church?* Downers Grove, IL: InterVarsity, 2012.

Bosch, David J. *Transforming Mission: Paradigm Shifts in Theology of Mission.* Maryknoll, NY: Orbis, 1991.

Bowlby, John. *Attachment.* Attachment and Loss 1. New York: Random House, 1997.

———. *The Making and Breaking of Affectional Bonds.* Abingdon, UK: Routledge, 2012.

Brewster, E. Thomas, and Elizabeth S. Brewster. *Bonding and the Missionary Task.* Pasadena, CA: Lingua House, 1982.

———. "Language Exploration and Acquisition Resource Notebook." *International Bulletin of Mission Research* 6.4 (1982) 160–64.

Brynjolfson, Rob. "Effective Equipping of the Cross-Cultural Worker." *Journal of the WEA Mission Commission*, January–April 2004, 72–79. https://www.worldevangelicals.org/resources/rfiles/res3_22_link_1282068370.pdf.

Caligiuri, Paula, and Ibraiz Tarique. "Predicting effectiveness in Global Leadership Activities." *Journal of World Business* 44 (2009) 336–46.

Claydon, David, "Context for the Production of the Lausanne Occasional Papers No. 44." In *The Two Thirds World Church*, edited by David D. Ruiz. Lausanne Occasional Paper 44. Lausanne Committee for World Evangelization, 2005.
Cook, Harold R. *Missionary Life and Work*. Chicago: Moody, 1959.
Custance, Arthur C. *Noah's Three Sons: Human History in Three Dimensions*. Grand Rapids: Zondervan, 1975.
Dayton, Edward R. *Mission Handbook: North American Protestant Ministries Overseas*. Monrovia, CA: MARC, 1976.
Demarest, Bruce A., and Keith J. Matthews. *Dictionary of Everyday Theology and Culture*. Colorado Springs, CO: NavPress, 2010.
"Do You Want to Bless Your Home? Follow These Steps." *Dot Property* (blog), March 7, 2016. https://www.dotproperty.com.ph/blog/how-to-have-your-new-home-blessed.
Dowsett, Rose. *Cape Town Commitment: A Confession of Faith and a Call to Action*. Peabody, MA: Hendrickson, 2012.
Farino, Lisa. "How happy Is Your City?" *MSN Health & Fitness*, July 14, 2011. http://health.msn.com/health-topics/depression/slideshow.aspx?cp-documentid=100173391&gt1=31036.
Ferris, Robert W. "Standards of Excellence in Missionary Training Centers." *Training* 1.1 (2000).
Fortosis, Steve. "Model for Understanding Cross-Cultural Morality." *Missiology* 18.2 (April 1990) 163–76.
Garrison, David. *Church Planting Movements: How God Is Redeeming a Lost World*. Midlothian, VA: WIGTake, 2004.
Ghosh, Iman. "Shape of the World, According to Old Maps." *Visual Capitalist*, July 12, 2019. https://www.visualcapitalist.com/shape-of-the-world-ancient-maps.
"Gidokgyo hwaksan'gwa segye gidokgyo byeonhwa" [Spread of Christianity and Change in the World Christianity]. *Pabalma*, Fall 2016. www.krim.org.
Glover, Robert Hall. *The Bible Basis of Missions*. Chicago: Moody, 1946.
Goodstein, Laurie. "Campus Crusade for Christ Is Renamed." *New York Times*, July 21, 2011, A:17.
Gration, John A. "Conversion in Cultural Context." *International Bulletin of Missionary Research* 7.4 (1983) 157–62.
Handy, Wesley L. "Correlating the Nevius Method with Church Planting Movements: Early Korean Revivals as a Case Study." *Eleutheria* 2.1 (2012). https://digitalcommons.liberty.edu/eleu/vol2/iss1/3.
Hendricks, Howard G. *Teaching to Change Lives*. Portland, OR: Multnomah, 1987.
Hendricks, Jurgens, and Chang-Dae Gwak. "Interpretation of the Recent Membership Decline in the Korean Protestant Church." *Missionalia: Southern African Journal of Mission Studies* 29.1 (April 2001) 55–68.
Henry, Tom. "It's All a Matter of Perspective. *Courier News*, September 9, 2017. https://www.tomhenry.org/2017/09/09/its-all-a-matter-of-perspective.
Hesselgrave, David. *Planting Churches Cross-Culturally*. Grand Rapids: Baker, 1980.
Hiebert, Paul G. *Anthropological Insights for Missionaries*. Grand Rapids: Baker, 1994.
———. "Critical Contextualization." *International Bulletin of Missionary Research* 11.3 (1987) 104–12.
———. *Transforming Worldviews: An Anthropological Understanding of How People Change*. Grand Rapids: Baker, 2008.

Houston, James M. *Memoirs of a Joyous Exile and Worldly Christian*. Eugene, OR: Cascade, 2019.
"How Does the School of Mission Work Best?" https://dci.org.uk/how-does-school-work-best.
Hull, Bill. *Disciple-Making Church*. Old Tappan, NJ: F.H. Revell, 1990.
———. *Jesus Christ, Disciplemaker*. Old Tappan, NJ: Revell, 1990.
Hunter, George G. *To Spread the Power*. Nashville: Abingdon, 1987.
Ilako, Cynthia. "Middle-Class Sinking in Debt as Bills Mount." *Star News*, April 11, 2019. https://www.the-star.co.ke/business/kenya/2019-04-12-middle-class-sinking-in-debt-as-bills-mount.
Im, Chandler H., and Amos Yong. *Global Diasporas and Mission*. Eugene, OR: Wipf & Stock, 2014.
ITAP International. "Culture in the Workplace Questionnaire Overview." http://www.itapintl.com/tools/culture-in-the-workplace-questionnaire-cw/itapcwquestionnaire.html.
Jang, Changil. "Is the Life of Korean Missionaries Exemplary? No." *PCK World*, January 20, 2009. http://www.pckworld.com/news/articleView.html?idxno=42353.
Johnson, Todd, and Gina A. Bellofatto. *Christianity in Its Global Context, 1970–2020 Society, Religion, and Mission*. South Hamilton, MA: Center for the Global Study of Christianity, 2013.
Kane, J. Herbert. *Understanding Christian Missions*. Grand Rapids: Baker, 1993.
Keller, Timothy. "Why Plant Churches?" http://download.redeemer.com/pdf/learn/resources/Why_Plant_Churches-Keller.pdf.
Kim, Myung Ho. "Dialogical Approach and Spiritual Growth: Discipleship Training in Korea." PhD diss., Trinity Evangelical Divinity School, 2006.
Kim, Sangkeun. "Sheer Numbers Do Not Tell the Entire Story." *Ecumenical Review* 57.4 (2005) 463–72.
Klaus, Marshall H., and John H. Kennell. *Maternal-Infant Bonding: The Impact of Early Separation or Loss on Family Development*. St. Louis, MO: Mosby, 1976.
Kraft, Charles H. *Anthropology for Christian Witness*. Maryknoll, NY: Orbis, 1996.
———. *Christianity in Culture*. Maryknoll, NY: Orbis, 1979.
———. *Communicating the Gospel God's Way*. Pasadena, CA: William Carey Library, 1983.
———. "Culture, Worldview and Contextualization." In *Perspectives on the World Christian Movement*, edited by Ralph D. Winter, 384–91. 3rd ed. Pasadena, CA: William Carey Library, 1999.
Landskroner, Ronald A. *The Nonprofit Manager's Resource Directory*. New York: Wiley, 2002.
Lane, Denis. *Tuning God's New Instruments*. Singapore: World Evangelical Fellowship, 1990.
Langmead, Ross. *Word Made Flesh: Towards an Incarnational Missiology*. Lanham, MD: University Press of America, 2004.
Larimore, Walt. "Poll Shows Sex within Marriage Is More Fulfilling." http://www.imom.com/poll-shows-sex-within-marriage-is-more-fulfilling.
Lee, Kwang Soon, and Young Won Lee. *Introduction to Missiology*. Seoul: Presbyterian, 1993.
Lee, Paul Sungro. "Impact of Missionary Training on Intercultural Readiness in Seoul, Korea." Ph.D. diss., Oxford Graduate School, 2014.

———. *Missionary Candidate Training*. Merrifield, VA: Evangelical Alliance for Preacher Training/Commission, 2008.
LeFever, Marlene D. *Learning Styles: Reaching Everyone God Gave You to Teach*. Colorado Springs, CO: David C. Cook, 1995.
Lewis, Jonathan. "Contextualizing Needs Assessment for Third World Missionary Training." *International Journal of Frontier Missions* 8.4 (1991) 121–26.
Lingenfelter, Judith E., and Sherwood G. Lingenfelter. *Teaching Cross-Culturally: An Incarnational Model for Learning and Teaching*. Grand Rapids: Baker, 2003.
Lingenfelter, Sherwood G., and Marvin Keene Mayers. *Ministering Cross-Culturally: An Incarnational Model for Personal Relationships*. Grand Rapids: Baker, 1986.
Loewen, Jacob Abram. *Culture and Human Values: Christian Intervention in Anthropological Perspective: Selections from the Writings*. Pasadena, CA: William Carey Library, 1975.
Lorenz, Konrad. "Der Kumpan in der Umwelt des Vogels: Der Artgenosse als auslösendes Moment sozialer Verhaltungsweisen." *Journal für Ornithologie* 83.2 (1935) 137–215; 83.3 (1935) 289–413.
Lutkehaus, Nancy. *Margaret Mead: Making of an American icon*. Princeton, NJ: Princeton University Press, 2008.
Malina, Bruce J. *Christian Origins and Cultural Anthropology: Practical Models for Biblical Interpretation*. Atlanta: John Knox, 1986.
Marshall, James P., and Elizabeth Wieling. "Promoting MFT Diversity through Cultural Plunges. *Family Therapy: The Journal of the California Graduate School of Family Psychology* 27.2 (2000) 89–99.
Matsumoto, David Ricky. *Cultural Influences on Research Methods and Statistics*. Pacific Grove, CA: Brooks/Cole, 1994.
McKinnon, Danny, and Andrew D. Cumbers. *Introduction to Economic Geography Globalization, Uneven Development and Place*. Abingdon, UK: Routledge, 2014.
"Missiological Abstracts." *Missionalia: Southern African Journal of Mission Studies* 11.2 (1983) 81–152.
Moon, Steve. "Missions from Korea 2016: Sustainability and Revitalization." *International Bulletin of Mission Research* 40.2 (2016) 181–85.
———. "Toward True Globalism in World Missions: Cross-Cultural Wisdom for a Polycentric Missions Reality." *Lausanne Global Analysis* 8.1 (January 2019). https://www.lausanne.org/content/lga/2019-01/toward-true-globalism-in-world-missions.
"More Time with Les and Pilar." https://www.dci.org.uk/main/moretime.htm.
Moreau, Scott A. "Contextualization: From an Adapted Message to an Adapted Life." In *The Changing Face of World Mission*, edited by Michael Pocock, Gailyn Van Rheenen, and Douglas McConnell, 329–32. Grand Rapids: Baker, 2005.
Morris, Thomas V. "Coherence of the Incarnation." In *Christian Apologetics: An Anthology of Primary Sources*, edited by Khaldoun A. Sweis, and Chad V. Meiste, 260–70. Grand Rapids: Zondervan, 2012.
Muller, Karl, Theo Sundermeier, Steven B. Bevans, and Richard H. Bliese, eds. *Dictionary of Mission: Theology, History, Perspectives*. Maryknoll, NY: Orbis, 1997.
Nida, Eugene A. *Message and Mission: The Communication of the Christian Faith*. Pasadena, CA: William Carey Library, 1960.
Noebel, David A. *Understanding the Times: The Religious Worldviews of Our Day and the Search for Truth*. Eugene, OR: Harvest, 1997.

Obenga, Theophile. "Egypt: Ancient History of African Philosophy." In *A Companion to African Philosophy*, edited by Kwasi Wiredu, 31. Oxford, UK: Blackwell, 2004.
Open Doors. "2020 World Watch List Report." https://www.opendoorsusa.org/2020-world-watch-list-report.
Pate, Larry D. "Changing Balance in Global Mission." *International Bulletin of Mission Research* 15.2 (1991) 56–61.
———. *From Every People: A Handbook of Two-Thirds World Missions with Directory, Histories, Analysis*. Monrovia, CA: Marc, 1989.
Piper, John. *Let the Nations Be Glad!: The Supremacy of God in Missions*. Grand Rapids: Baker, 2010.
Reed, Lyman E. *Preparing Missionaries for Intercultural Communication: A Bicultural Approach*. Pasadena, CA: William Carey Library, 2000.
Reisacher, Evelyne Annick. "Processes of Attachment between the Algerians and French within the Christian Community in France." PhD diss., Fuller Theological Seminary, 2001.
Reyburn, William D. "Identification in the Missionary Task." *Practical Anthropology* 1 (1960) 1–15.
Richard, Ramesh. "Training of Pastors: A High Priority for Global Ministry Strategy." *Lausanne Global Analysis* 4.5 (September 2015). https://www.lausanne.org/content/lga/2015-09/training-of-pastors.
Rodewald, Mike. "Barriers to the Gospel: Approaching Contextualisation from a Confessional Lutheran Perspective." *Missio apostolica* 22.1 (2014) 54–62.
Rohde, Douglas L. T. "On the Common Ancestors of All Living Humans." *American Journal of Physical Anthropology* (2003).
Sanders, J. Oswald. *Spiritual Leadership*. Chicago: Moody, 1980.
Sanneh, Lamin O. *Whose Religion Is Christianity?: The Gospel beyond the West*. Grand Rapids: Eerdmans, 2003.
Schein, Edgar H. *Organizational Culture and Leadership*. San Francisco: Jossey-Bass, 1985.
Schore, Allan N. "Attachment and the Regulation of the Right Brain." *Attachment and Human Development* 2.1 (2000) 23–47.
Smalley, William A. "Cultural Implications of an Indigenous Church." In *Perspectives on the World Christian Movement: A Reader*, edited by Ralph D. Winter and Steven C. Hawthorne, 494–502. Pasadena, CA: William Carey Library, 1981.
Song, Minho. "Contextualization and Discipleship." *Evangelical Review of Theology* 30.3 (2006) 249–63.
Sroufe, L. Alan. "Coherence of Individual Development: Early Care, Attachment, and Subsequent Developmental Issues." *American Psychologist* 34.10 (1979) 834–41.
Stutzman, Linford. "Incarnational Approach to Mission in Modern, Affluent Societies." *Urban Mission* 8 (1991) 35–43.
Theological Education Fund. *Ministry in Context: The Third Mandate Programme of the Theological Education Fund 1970–1977*. Bromley, UK: TEF, 1972.
Tilley, Keith. *Mission America: Wesleyan Perspective*. Morrisville, NC: Lulu Com, 2012.
Van Meter, Jim. "US Report of Findings on Missionary Retention." WEA Resources, December 2003. http://www.worldevangelicals.org/resources/view.htm?id=95.
Velick, Bruce. *Joy!: Photographs of Life's Happiest Moments*. San Francisco: Chronicle, 2019.

Wakatama, Pius. *Independence for the Third World Church: An African's Perspective on Missionary Work*. Downers Grove, IL: InterVarsity, 1976.

Weightman, Daniel A. "Defining the Essential Components of Indigenization: A Roadmap for Parachurch Mission Agencies Serving the Bahamas." PhD diss., Reformed Theological Seminary, 2008.

West, Russell W. "The Re-Eventing of Theological Education: Toward a Pedagogy of Leadership Formation in the Verbomoteur Mode." Paper presented at the International Orality Network Forum in Asbury Theological Seminary, Wilmore, KY, 2014.

Wilberforce, William. *Real Christianity*. Ventura, CA: Regal, 2006.

Wood, Wendy, and Alice H. Eagly. "A Cross-Cultural Analysis of the Behavior of Women and Men: Implications for the Origins of sex Differences." *Psychological Bulletin* 128.5 (2002) 699–727.

Woodbridge, John D. *Great Leaders of the Christian Church*. Chicago: Moody, 1988.

World Evangelical Alliance. "ReMAP II: Worldwide Missionary Retention Study and Best Practices." WEA Resources, February 24, 2010. http://www.worldevangelicals.org/resources/rfiles/res3_96_link_1292358945.pdf.

Wu, Jackson. *One Gospel for All Nations: A Practical Approach to Biblical Contextualization*. Pasadena, CA: William Carey Library, 2015.

Yohannan, K. P. *Revolution in World Missions*. Carrollton, TX: GFA, 2004.

Youssef, Michael. *Leadership Style of Jesus*. Eugene, OR: Harvest, 2013.

Zaimov, Stoyan. "S. Korean Megachurch Pastor Loses Case in Leadership Fight; Church Opposes Court Involvement." *Christian Post*, December 2018. http://www.christianpost.com/news/s-korean-megachurch-pastor-loses-case-in-leadership-fight-church-opposes-court-involvement.html.

Zurlo, Gina A. "World as 100 Christians." *Gordon Conwell Theological Seminary*, January 29, 2020. https://www.gordonconwell.edu/blog/100christians.

Subject Index

Abrahamic blessing, 16–18, 56
accountability, 18, 68, 75, 133, 136, 145
   acculturation, 35, 50, 54, 67,
      76–77, 108, 118–119, 121, 126,
      128
Acts, book of, 56–58, 86–87
Adam, 13, 83, 122
Adeney, Miriam, 22
anointing with oil, 108, 112–113
anthropologist, 72, 105
anthropology
   biblical, 51
   cultural, 102
   on lineage of ancestor, 51–52, 64
apologetics, 87
apostles, choosing of, 30, 60
attitudes, 15, 31, 52, 73, 121, 126–127,
   130, 142
authority, 39, 102–103, 133, 154
Azariah, V.S., 126, 137

Babel, 50
Babylon, 50
balance
   in contextualization, 107–108
   in discipleship, 4, 36, 156
   in global mission, 71
   of wealth, 17
behavioral science, 5, 51, 72, 83, 85, 88,
   94, 103, 127
Bible, the
   on places in different names, 50
   on the fall, 90

   on the kingdom, 9–10, 17–18, 57,
      60, 79, 85, 150–153
bicultural community, 74
blessing
   Biblical definition of, 17–18
   of missionary, 10, 14–15, 152
bonding versus going native, 125
Borthwick, Paul, 76

Cain, 120
Campus Crusade for Christ. See Cru.
catholicity, 100, 113
challenging and confronting a culture,
   45, 96, 127
Christian elders, 33, 39, 99–100
church
   and Peter's confession, 156
   growth, 6, 63–64
   leader, 19, 25, 134, 136, 140, 144
   planting, 20–21, 36–37, 39–42
church construction
   and issue of control, 140
   conflict, 139
   funding, 142–143
   model, 140–143
   principle, 143–144
   style, 140–142
Church Planting Movements, 40
city/town
   biblical model of expanding from,
      54
   setting ministry base, 49–50
Coca-Cola, 48
commandments, 93, 102

commitment, expression of, 127
community
    adjusting and belonging to, 54, 73
    function of, 17, 68, 140
    importance of, 143
    needs of, 49, 126
    transformation, 40, 154–155
companionship
    and cooperation, 144–145
    over cross-cultural difference, 129
Confucius, 92
contextualization
    and incarnation, 98, 105, 108, 120–123
    challenge of, 103–107
    cultural, 78, 134, 142
    danger of, 100, 107–108
    examples of, 110–113
    exegetical, 104
    for community, 108–109
    inevitability of, 104–105
    principle of, 106–107
conversion, 6–7, 69, 143
creation, 83, 122–123, 148, 155
creation and evolution, 90
Creative Access Regions, the, 49
cross-cultural communication
    and learning curves, 4–5
    expression, 4–5, 94–95, 109
    noise, 95
    of gospel, 95–96
    principle, 88, 95–96
    sensitivity, 94, 106
cross-cultural propaganda, 49–50, 54–55
Cru, 3
cult, 39, 48–49
culture
    adapting to the, 35, 50, 54, 67, 76–77, 108, 118–119, 121, 126, 128
    and confrontation, 53
    another, 13, 104–105, 123
    channel of motivation and, 52
    counter, 45, 100
    foreign, 67, 94, 107
    of the East, 87–88
    of the West, 87–88, 134
    origin of, 51, 99, 108
    sub-, 151
cultural
    blindness, 88
    conflict, 109, 102–103
    difference, 76, 94
    diversity, 78–79
    hybridity, 14, 65, 86
    merit, 71, 79
    mono-, 102, 149–150, 156
    multi-, 78–79, 86–87, 103
    zones, 52–53, 92–93
cultural gospel and contextualized gospel, 78

daughter church, 37, 39–48, 156
De Chardin, Pierre, 8
deceptive motivation for mission, 129
development, 23, 99
developmental psychology and missiology, 72, 74
devotion to God's kingdom, 9–10
diaspora, 14, 86–87, 149
different level of commitment for missions, 3
discipleship
    and bonding, 119–120, 126
    and family life, 151–152
    and Great Commission, 102, 158
    and waiting, 131
    cross-cultural, 34–41, 51–52, 84
    failure case, 37–39
    multiplication, 24, 41–45, 156
    self-replication, 96
    success case, 36–37, 121–122
diversity
    addressing, 151
    of cultures, 6, 13
dynamic equivalence churches, 105–106

EAPTC. See Evangelical Alliance for Preacher Training/Commission.
early church, 17, 59, 86, 128, 149
ecclesial impact, 149
Egypt, 50, 86
elders, Christian, 33, 39, 99–100
empirical research/Wilcoxon, 66

Ephesus, 33, 134, 156
ethnocentrism, 65, 88
ethnorelativism, 65
Europe, secularization of, 149
Evangelical Alliance for Preacher Training/Commission, 19–20, 24–25, 33, 41–42, 48–55, 66, 77, 145, 150–151, 154, 156
evangelicals, 156
evangelism, 57, 60
evangelism and mission, 157
exile, 86

faith
   integration of culture and, 100, 105
   vision and, 24, 154
faithfulness, 36–37, 67–68, 133
family,
   as building block for missionary commission, 151–152
   bonding for cross-cultural preparation, 67
female genital mutilation, 92
financial resources, 86, 126, 129, 143–145, 152–153
future of mission, 149–150

Garrison, David, 40
generations of discipleship, 39–45, 46–48
Genesis 12, 16–18, 56
global
   church, 64–65, 76, 78–79
   ministry expansion, 23–25
   north, 63, 76
   south, 63–64, 70–71
globalization and mission force, 62, 76, 78–79, 149
glocal, 150
Glover, Robert Hall, 142
God
   calling people to mission, 4, 13, 29, 62–63, 65, 76, 78, 91, 129, 148–150, 157–158
   image of, 83, 90, 92, 123, 155
   kingdom of, 9–10, 17–18, 57, 60, 79, 85, 149–153
   knowing better through maturity, 46, 69–71, 91–92, 102, 118
   leading of, 6, 10, 58–60
   long-suffering of, 14–15, 18–19
   love of, 6–7, 152
   mission of. See mission of God.
   promise and fulfillment, 16, 23–24, 47–48, 154
   sovereignty of, 20–21, 57–58, 88
gods of heaven and earth, 110–111
gospel
   and cultural application, 53, 94–96, 98–103, 104–105, 109, 143
   and the Holy Spirit, 57
   contextualization and, 64, 78, 87, 98–100, 105, 109, 143
   incarnation and, 34–35, 72, 87, 119–123, 130–131
   religiosity versus, 89
   worldview shift and, 91–92
Gunter, Nina, 153
Gutmann, Bruno, 123

heresy, See cult.
Hesselgrave, David J., 136–137
Hiebert, Paul, 69, 74, 98
hindrances to missionary discipleship, 128–131
Holy Spirit, the
   and speaking through church leadership, 140, 144
   fellowship with, 58–60
   leading mission, 23, 25, 48, 157
   mission and, 148
   role of, 56–57, 62–63, 56
   waiting on, 37
homogenization, 45–46, 51–52, 72, 76, 113, 120–128
house church, 14, 24–25
humility, 35, 125, 130, 142
Hunter, George, 98

idolatry, 69–70
IGSL. See International Graduate School of Leadership.
imago Dei. See image of God.

incarnation
  and colonialism, 121–122, 130–131
  and contextualization, 98, 105, 108, 120–123
  and humility, 75, 142
  and ministry style, 128
  and missionary's living cost, 118–119, 127–128
  and understanding, 122
  of funding, 142
  of Jesus Christ, 62, 72–73, 100–101, 119, 122, 124–125, 142, 155, 157
individualism, 103
integrity in the gospel, 96
intercultural readiness
  components of, 67, 76–77
  training for, 66–68, 75
international church planting, 49–52
International Graduate School of Leadership, 5, 25, 78–79, 109, 111, 154–157
interpersonal relationship, 19, 34–35, 65, 67, 75–77
Israel, 50, 88

Jerusalem, 29, 62, 88, 148–149
Jesus Christ
  on discipleship, 30, 60, 133, 155
  on following the call, 13, 157
  on incarnation, 35, 62, 72–73, 94, 100–101, 122, 125, 155
  on leading mission, 62, 78, 148, 157
  on similar kind less friction, 46
Jews
  Abrahamic blessing and, 16
  Gentiles and, 16
  scattered, 86–87, 149
John, the Gospel of, 59

Kane, J. Herbert, 125
kingdom, the, 9–10, 17–18, 57, 60, 79, 85, 149–153
knowing about missions versus knowing missions, 3
Kraft, Charles, 34, 72–74

Lane, Denis, 71
language, 5, 49–50, 53–55, 73, 87, 95, 124, 127, 143
launching new churches, 23, 40–42, 48, 154, 156
Lausanne Covenant, 52–53, 63, 149
leadership
  cross-cultural, 49, 78–79, 83–84
  development, 33, 126
  succession, 33
learning
  of culture, 4–5, 19, 74
  through previous experience, 65–67, 76
  through small-group, 68, 76, 155–157
limited resources, 76
Lingenfelter, Sherwood G., 72–73
local church
  and cross-cultural discipleship, 103
  and kingdom, 140
  empowering, 156
Lord
  hand of, 6–8, 15, 33, 57–58, 140
  servant of, 31–32, 58, 62, 78
love
  and discipleship, 31, 35, 101, 152
  and friendship, 126
Luther, Martin, 100

Majority World, the, 35, 65–66, 70–71, 76–77, 118–119, 133
Mayers, Marvin Keene, 72–73
MCT. See *Missionary Candidate Training*.
Mead, Margaret, 155
mentoring, 30–35, 47, 102, 132–133, 156–157
migration, 4–5, 51, 54, 67, 86
ministry
  base, 23–24, 58–59
  expansion, 23–24, 39–45, 48–50, 54–55, 66, 151, 155–156
missio Dei, the
  and cultural hybridity, 86
  and Great Commission, 149–150
  and imago Dei, 123
  holistic approach of, 118

meaning of, 25
missiology, 72–73, 101, 109, 122, 134, 148–149
mission agency, 19, 75–76
missional life, 56, 60, 85–86, 88, 91, 150–158
missionary
    and open mind, 126
    cost of, 14
    family issue of, 75, 119, 151–152
    global ratio of, 64–65
    life, 120–121, 124
    recruitment of, 24–25, 156–157
    training of, 66–77
Missionary Candidate Training, 66–76
mixed nature of culture, 86–86, 150–151
models
    of incarnational living, 73–75, 118–122, 125–128, 155
    of church construction, 140–143
    of discipleship multiplication, 46–47, 68–69, 149–150, 156
mother church, 39–48, 54, 156
movement(s)
    Church Planting Movement, 40
    of cultural group, 54–55, 75
    of Korean missionary, 23–25
    of world missions, 23–25, 48

natural church planting, 42, 156
Noebel, David, 69
non-Western,
    church building, 141–142
    worldview, 69–71, 76–77

organization, church, 37, 48–49
order,
    of map direction, 87
    of necessities, 87–88
ownership, 144

partnership. See companionship.
pastor
    and biblical mission, 130
    ceremonial duty, 108, 111–113
    multicultural, 103

    on gradual contextualization, 99–100
    on mission involvement, 77
pastoral support, 58
Pate, Larry D., 70–71
paternalism, 76, 130, 132–138
Paul, apostle
    on adaptation, 124, 145–146
    and church planting, 39–40
    and cultural hybridity, 86–87
    and Mark, 31
Pauline cycle, 136–137
personalized mentoring, 29–32, 152, 156
Perspectives on the World Christian Movement, 70
Peter, apostle, 87, 156
Peterson, Chris, 10
Piper, John, 102
polygamy, 90
poor, the
    due to imbalance, 17
    helping, 17–18, 39
postmodernism, 69, 88, 99
prayer meetings, 37, 58
preacher, 19–20, 29, 94, 108, 154–155
preaching, 29, 35–36, 77–78, 99–100, 118, 136, 143, 149
prosperity gospel, 38, 134
pride, 129–130
psychology, 72–74

race
    and culture, 83
    and reconciliation, 103, 109
    biblical definition, 83
    conflict of, 90
    origin and development, 51–53
racism. See tribalism.
reconciliation
    and unity, 36, 48, 58
    tribal, 49
redemptive history, 63, 86–88, 157
Reed, Lyman, 93
reincarnation, 92
relationship(s)
    and cross-cultural discipleship, 96
    changed by priority setting, 156

relationship(s) (continued)
    of missionary and local people, 34–35, 45, 51–52, 67, 75, 92, 113–114, 118–131, 134
relic veneration, 113
repentance, 58
respect for cultural sensitivity, 66, 76, 94, 106
restoration, 123
Revolution in World Missions, 135

status
    of European Church, 78, 149
    of global Christianity, 64–65
    of the Church of Korea, 6, 24–25, 111
sacrifice, 9, 31, 35, 79, 102, 124, 152, 157
salvation
    of nations, 152, 154, 157
    through preaching, 29, 77–78, 152
sanctification, 56, 118, 134
Sarang Community Church, 3–4
self-care, 93–94
self-centeredness, 88, 157
selfless dedication to God, 9, 12–13
servant-steward leader, 126, 154–155
sexual fulfillment
    and marriage, 89–90
    and porn phenomenon, 89–90, 93–94
    higher for Christian couples, 89–90
short-term mission, 18, 77, 145, 151
similar kind less friction, 45–46, 52, 108, 113, 127
sin
    and cultural zones, 52–53, 93, 96
    temptation of, 7
slavery, 86, 134
small group
    multiplication, 155
    multiplication stages, 46–48
social outreach, 49
sociology, 65, 72, 105
sound contextualization, 99–100, 108–109
Southern Baptist Convention, 40
sovereignty of God, 20–21, 57–58, 88

stagnancy, 58
stewardship, 18, 124, 130, 136, 138, 146
Studd, C.T., 9
succeeding leadership, 32–33
suicide, 92
syncretism, 107

Table of Nations, 51–52, 122–123
team ministry, 78–79
theological
    consideration, 51–52, 122, 132
    training, 96, 156
Third World, the. See the Majority World.
time orientation versus event orientation, 95
together-in-difference, 125
tracing the call of life, 13
transformation, 8, 20, 40, 63, 89, 107, 122, 154–157
translation, 66, 104–105, 122
transliteration, 104–105
tribalism, 52, 92
Trinity, the, 62–63
Two Thirds-World, the. See the Majority World.

Unreached People Groups, 42, 149
urban suburbs, 39–40, 43, 54, 103, 118–119
urbanization, 39–40, 54

vision
    and movements, 23–25, 54, 150–151
    and world mission, 12, 57–58
    casting of, 21, 23, 52, 77, 87, 92, 126, 132–133

Wakatama, Pius, 134–135
West, Russell, 99
Western,
    church building, 139, 141–142
    worldview, 71, 87–88, 95, 119, 125, 134
Wilberforce, William, 134
Winter, Ralph, 70

wisdom and the word, 10, 39
witness(es)
 in the Revelation, 101
 lifestyle of, 56, 150–152
Woodbridge, John D., 145
world map shifts, 84–85
worldview
 difference(s), 69, 83
 power of, 85–86
 self-image and, 89, 93–94
 shifts, 69–71
 Stephen's sermon in Acts and, 86

training, 69–71, 89–92
transformation, 69–70, 91–92
worship
 facility, 111, 139, 140, 143–144, 156
 style, 5, 37
Wu, Jackson, 107

Yohannan, K.P., 135–136
Yong, Amos, 14
Youssef, Michael, 141

www.ingramcontent.com/pod-product-compliance
Lightning Source LLC
Chambersburg PA
CBHW051057160426
43193CB00010B/1219